Behind My Glorious Smile

Behind My Glorious Smile

Antoinette Thomas

TURN THE PAGE
IN YOUR LIFE

First Edition

Cover Design By: Antoinette Thomas & Owen Watson, Ph.D.

Editor: Ramona L. Watson, Ph.D.

Library of Congress Cataloging-in-Publication Data

ISBN-9781733164146

Dedicated to my children who are my strength, and my main reasons for wanting to be better in every aspect.

Contents

Foreword

<><><><><>

If there was ever a smile that could light up any room, Antoinette is the possessor of that genuine, glamorous smile. With a complementary exuberant attitude, it is seemingly impossible to perceive her as ever having had a troubled life. That is, until you read this candid autobiography, penned by Antoinette, which details the calamitous life she endured.

Moving from big city, Chicago, to small town, Blytheville, was supposed to help keep her on track for a bright future. However, Blytheville would be the place where she would face palpable dangers during her teenage years. She suffered rape, promiscuity, depression, suicidal tendencies, a miscarriage and being a teen mom – all at a very young age. She struggled to survive tremendous mental, physical, and emotional abuse. But through God's love and mercy coupled with her faith, she prevailed beyond the perceived stigma of society.

Antoinette's story is one of perseverance and determination; she refused to be an accepter of defeat or a helpless victim. For inspiring others, she exercises faith for living a better life and sharing the beauty God has brought forth from the ashes – her testimony! The following pages of *Behind My*

Glorious Smile are sure to open eyes to the presence of a faithful, merciful, and loving God, who is able to renew and restore beyond any level of chaos. As Antoinette continues gaining clarity about God, she makes necessary adjustments for mirroring a lifestyle that represents Him well!

~Owen Watson, Ph.D.~

Introduction

◇◇◇◇◇◇

M y journey through life has led me down many unwanted paths – promiscuity, suicidal thoughts, rape, depression, and teen pregnancy, just to name a few. In each of those obstacles, I have had to face unpleasant emotions and consequences that I was not prepared for. During those times, although I did not realize it until later, the grace of God was positioned to protect and catapult me as an overcomer of each hurdle. Each hurdle that was designed to either stagnate or destroy me was used by God in making me.

It is hard for many to give glory to God, frankly because they do not know God. It is not so much that they do not believe in His existence (which most do), it's that they don't know Him intimately. I come to understand that knowing God intimately comes by having that personal relationship Him whereby you surrender wholeheartedly all the weights of pride, doing things "my way", regrets, detrimental thoughts, bad habits, and unforgiveness in exchange for the essential presence of Him in your everyday life.

As you can see…

Teen pregnancy

Suicidal thoughts

Contemplated abortion

Promiscuity

Rape

Miscarriage

Depression

…yesterday's journey was not easy, but it became the overcoming testimony of God's favor in my life today. After being pregnant at 14, having 3 children by 3 different men, and not having a college degree – His death and resurrection, yet, made me worthy of His mercy and grace. I now have that unspeakable joy and courage to share my testimony! If you do not know my story, it's impossible for you to understand me being His glory. Many people question my thoughts, my values, and my godly lifestyle NOW, but if you knew what I have BEEN through, you would know why I operate the way I do now. I DO NOT think I am better than anybody, I just choose NOT to go back to those places that GOD has delivered me from. As a believer, I expect to be hunted by devil, but I refuse to be haunted by condemnation.

The purpose for this book is to share my testimony in hopes of encouraging others who are hopelessly and helplessly wandering or questioning "why should I keep moving forward?" I want them to know that their current circumstances are not permanent, and trouble truly does not last always. They need to know that their testimony is being formed for a much bigger purpose than they could ever imagine; and they can't afford to lie dormant. The very thing they are made to overcome is the very thing that, once shared, will save the lives of many.

"The pain that you've been feeling, can't compare to the joy that's coming!"

Chapter 1

Innocent Little One

◇◇◇◇◇◇◇◇◇

As the adage goes "children will be children." However, sociocultural factors heavily influence what types of children are produced. We are born innocent and molded by impressions encountered throughout life – whether 'good' or 'bad', 'right' or 'wrong', etc. What keeps children from being children are circumstances far beyond their realm of responsibility – there was no exemption for me.

As far back as I can remember, the normalcy of life as I had known it may not have been perfect, but it was fun filled. After all, isn't that how it's meant to be for children – FUN?! Children should not have to worry about 'grown-up' business, and never ever should they be made to 'mentally' grow faster than they ought to. However, as impromptu circumstances occur, life abruptly changes in an instant and comes with ripple effects that affects everyone in various ways.

I am an Illinois child, born in Chicago, best known worldwide as the 'Windy City' and by the natives as 'Chiraq' (due to extreme crime, violence, and shameful injustices). Although Chicago had and has its flaws, as a child, I was pretty well shielded by the love of family. My parents are Anthony, also known as Tony, and Brigette. They are both Chicagoans who met through my uncle Randall, my mother's brother. They all lived in the same neighborhood. When my parents first met, they were dating other people. As chance would have it, they started dating one another years later after their breakups from previous relationships.

My mom is such a beautiful person inside and out. Thirty plus years after my birth, and she still has the looks and spirit of a teenager – timelessly aging. She is the life of any party and always sought out as a travel partner for vacations and cruises by family members. Dad is the epitome of what any woman would and should seek in a man. He's very handsome (I'm not just saying that because he's my dad, it's really true), speaks from the heart as a straight shooter, intelligent, and caring. From what I was told, there was a strong 'puppy love' between the two of them, to the extent that both sides of their families were rooting for them to marry and live happily ever after. Although their love for one another produced me in 1988 (mom was 21 and dad was 19), down the road of life, their being married and living happily ever after was not in the cards.

Nevertheless, in addition to living in Chicago, I have also lived in Evanston and Waukegan, but I do not recall much about living in those locations. The extent of living in Evanston, as much as I can remember, is going to school (1st grade) and living in a large two-story house with a basement, that's about it. Whereas living in Waukegan, I have absolutely no recollection.

Sadly, as I reflect, I never lived in a two-parent home with my biological parents [Tony and Brigette]. What has been revealed to me is that they were together until I was about two years old. Did it affect me during that time? I can't say for sure; I was too young to understand. But I am certain that the long-term effect of not having both biological parents in the home set the stage for having a weak foundation and affected my future in some ways. Even though it was either one or the other parent present at any given time, I was never left nor felt lonely as an only child. Whatever time spent with either parent was always grand and exciting.

Although separated, my parents were very fun-loving and caring. They bought me lots of toys and they actually took time to play with me, despite whatever 'grown-up' things going on in their personal lives – memories I will forever cherish. Additionally, on both sides of their families, I had grandparents who spoiled me and cousins who were my company for entertainment. Because I was so young and never lived with my mother and father as a couple in the same house, their separation did not affect my routine of having fun as a young child.

Around the age of five, another father figure came into my life. He was my mom's boyfriend and, ironically, his name was Tony. I remember Tony as a pretty nice guy and considered him a father figure because he had a serious relationship with my mom and treated me well - as if I was his biological daughter. I am not sure if there was ever any beef between he and my biological Dad. If so, I have never personally witnessed any animosity portrayed by either toward the other.

Around the age of six, life as an only child was starting to come to an end. Like most children, as I would expect, my emotions were a mixture of jealousy and happiness. My Mom and biological Dad had moved forward in their separate lives by creating families with other partners. It seemed as though in the blink of an eye I suddenly had three siblings. My mother had given birth to my sister, Shacora (aka Cora), in 1994 which was followed by the birth of my brother, Dontel (aka Man-Man) two years later (1996). They were and still are too adorable and high-spirited. Nothing about their character or youthfulness has changed over the past 20 plus years – it must be hereditary from our mother. In 1997, my dad fathered my sister, Toni, with his new love interest. Toni is pretty laid back [mellow] with a great sense of humor. I think my dad, Toni, and I all inherited that smooth type of personality from my father's mother (Ruth Thomas, aka 'grandma').

Between 1990 and 1996, we were constantly moving and living in either Chicago or Blytheville [a small town in Arkansas]. As a child, I found the frequent relocations to be exciting and explorative. The only memorable major issue I recall having were the continual switching of schools, routines, and living arrangements between Chicago and Blytheville during 3rd to 5Th grades. Surprisingly, throughout the inconsistent lifestyle, my grades remained steady [i.e., good] without missing a beat.

During those numerous moves, it became difficult to form a tighter bond with all of my siblings whom I loved dearly. I was either with my mom and two half siblings or with my father, stepsister [Toni], and my father's love interest's [Tiffany] daughter, Briana. But as far as all of us being together, it rarely ever happened. We all still managed to make the best of whatever time we had together without regret.

Chapter 2

Grandmothers' Love

◇◇◇◇◇◇◇◇◇◇

In the course of the frequent moves, I distinctly remember living at Grandma Ruth's house in Chicago. Grandma had a soft voice, and she was definitely sweet and sassy. I had not experienced her sassiness until I was much older. She was always happy and full of so much joy and life. Her mind was always much sharper than mine when it came to remembering things – she would later reminisce and tease me about it in my teenage years. She was a widow – her husband, Grandpa Willie, passed away in 1994. I do not recall knowing much about him.

She lived in a one-level brick house with a large basement. There were three bedrooms, a medium-sized fenced yard, a front porch with stairs, an enclosed porch on the rear of the house, and detached garage near the alley. I spent many times there climbing trees and fences, playing in the basement, and babysitting the iguana that lived next door. You read that correctly, I was playing with an iguana! The iguana was green, roughly two feet long and seemed to weigh no more than eight pounds. I'm sure he loved me because I fed him lettuce and carried him around like a baby whenever the opportunity presented itself.

I was always a rather curious kid but never pushed the limits too much. That childlike curiosity would serve as a detrimental precursor to life ahead. I was not one to settle on living life "within a box." As a youngster, I've always had the notion that space, outside the realm of who and what I knew, was something to be explored. There seemed to have always been something innate desiring inquisitiveness and going against the grain. Now, understand that some of those inquisitive ventures were great and others not so much. Case in point – one day my father had specifically told my cousin Jazmine (who was about three years younger than I) and me not to touch any of the medications in the medicine cabinet. Well, my cousin dared me to take some pills (which turned out to be Tylenol) and, although I knew better, I accepted the challenge and took a couple of pills anyway. Somehow, my father knew it was tampered with; I'm not sure how he knew but he knew. Well, the consequences were being disciplined in the form of the old-fashioned 'butt whooping' along with an explanation of the dangers of taking any type of pills that are not specifically prescribed for me, bought over the counter by me, or given to me by a parent. After the discipline [i.e., butt whooping], I realized that my feelings were hurt more than my butt and I'm quite sure he was hurt even more than I. Years later, while talking with him about the incident, he didn't remember it occurring. Either old age has set in and affected his memory, or he prefers to remember the good times only. Whatever the reason for his 'amnesia', I clearly remember it as being a valuable lesson learned and a mistake that was never repeated.

All in all, my time staying at Grandma Ruth's house served up so many good memories, including birthday parties with clowns (not the creepy ones), going fishing with my uncle, playing dress-up, making up dance routines with my sister and cousin, and putting together talent shows in the kitchen for everyone to enjoy. We used things such as hairbrushes and television remotes as microphones during our singing acts. Amusingly, we were somewhat the innovative fashion designers. We would make dresses out of sheets and put on fashion shows in the living room. The sheets were old. I do not particularly recall Grandma ever fussing at us about being in her sheets – it was all in sheer fun. I'm sure Grandma had new sheets – and we for sure knew which ones were off-limits. Whoever was in the house at the time received an invitation to the fashion shows as well as talent shows - sometimes written, other times verbal. Family members were always supportive by attending.

My grandma [Ruth] was a very sweet and caring lady. She would make us big, nice breakfasts on the weekends and, believe you me, she knew exactly how to 'throw down' in the kitchen! With her being maybe five feet tall, I would always compare our heights. It made me feel good to know I was growing, although at that age I hadn't realized that at some point in life, the older you get you start losing height – so I was really winning in growth by default.

Another fun memory at Grandma's house involved my dad and a mouse. I laugh just thinking about it as I am writing. Living where we were in Chicago, it was common to come across mice, whether in the streets or in the house. One thing many people, including Grandma, kept in stock was mice poison to help deter and control the infestations. It was carefully placed in key locations where mice might and/or would enter the house or be found seeking food. Everyone in the house was aware of where the poison was planted and, us children were specifically told to stay clear of it. Well, there was a mouse that had eaten some of the poison and was frantically running in circles in front of Grandma's bedroom before it abruptly died. Out of her fear of mice [musophobia], Grandma hurriedly barricaded herself in her bedroom. She was not the only mice fearing person in the house, we all were. Anyway, Dad, being extremely terrified of mice, offered to pay me $10 to get rid of it by taking it to the dumpster located in the alley located behind the house. Although I too was just as terrified as everyone else, whatever fear I had was bought in exchange for that $10! Yes, this sister [me] did what she had to do – afraid, but, with motivation; motivated by getting the $10 and afraid of passing up that opportunity. That was the easiest and quickest $10 I have ever made.

Interestingly, I had no qualms about playing with an iguana, but I feared mice and rabbits. You read it correctly: R-A-B-B-I-T-S! I was so afraid of them that I was literally scared to go play on the back porch because my sister Briana had a creepy rabbit she had kept there. I do not remember his name, nor do I care to. To me, what made that rabbit so creepy was the fact that every time I would see it on the porch, no matter what time of day or night, it was always awake and staring at me. I even questioned my family on whether or not rabbits ever sleep. Just creepy!!!

Another favorite hangout place of mine while living in Chicago was my great grandmother's house. For some reason or another, all generations of grandmothers have a knack for bringing people together with peace and fun. She was my Mom's grandmother, and her name was Annie (the same as her eldest daughter, my grandmother) but everyone called her "Ballie" because she would dress and act like a clown with and for the children; however, I was one of the few to call her "Big Ma" instead of "Ballie." Big Ma served as a foster parent to many kids, mostly boys, so there was always someone around my age to play with. Across the street from her house was a playground and living next door to her was my best friend, Brittany, who was around my age and living with her grandmother, Mrs. Fisher.

While at Big Ma's house, finding something to do for fun was never a problem and it was mostly free. There were times when my friend Brittany and I would take Mrs. Fisher's pots into the backyard and make mud pies – and, of course, NO, we did not eat any of them. I do not know if Mrs. Fisher ever cared about us using the pots, but I'm thinking probably not because we did it very often. Another pastime favorite of mine at Big Ma's house was playing video games in the basement with the boys [fostered children]. I considered them as my cousins, except the one I had a crush on. His name was Jeremy, and he resembled the rapper, actor, and poet Tupac Shakur. I forget his age, but he was a little older than I. We were way too young for anything other than having feelings of a minor crush, but I really just thought he was cute.

Big Ma was hilarious even in times of her being serious. For instance, to control the portions of snacks and cereal we children ate, she would keep the items in her bedroom. We would have to bring our bowls in the mornings for her to ration out the cereal proportionately. Something totally humorous occurred when Big Ma had a can of pop [i.e., "soda" for the southerners] sitting on a table. One of her foster kids really wanted that drink.

Eventually he took it upon himself to deviously get the drink. Oh, he achieved the impossible; however, he was not ready for the consequences. Little to any of our knowledge at the time, what he ingested was not pop at all – it was a can full of Big Ma's mucus and spit. Yes, it was too disgusting but too funny for the rest of us kids not to laugh nor feel sorry for him. Those memorable times at Big Ma's house will forever be treasured, as will she.

Chapter 3

Blytheville Beginnings

◇◇◇◇◇◇◇◇◇◇◇

I did not experience life without my biological father until my mom, along with my siblings and I, permanently moved to Arkansas in 1996 when I was approximately 8 years old. The daily physical interactions between my father and I may have been hampered but his love and support were ongoing. To this day, he continues to maintain a steady presence in my life and always assures and instills in me how beautiful I am. He yet supports and inspires me to be the best I can in living life. He refuses to ever be a black, stereotyped, uninvolved, status quo father.

How did we go from Chicago to small town Blytheville? Good question, but to be quite honest with you, I do not know for certain. However, what I know and can speculate on is that members from my mother's side of the family had made the move from Chicago to Blytheville in the early 1980's. Afterward, my grandparents and mother, along with us children, followed suit.

With constantly having to move becoming a way of life, I unconsciously developed a desensitization to being separated from my father and Chicago family when we moved permanently to Blytheville. Quite honestly, as a child I never viewed nor handled it as a "we'll never see one another again" situation. Did I want to leave my Chicago family? Not necessarily, but unknowingly at the time, God was readying me for what was needed in my life by way of my mother's parents (my grandparents - Annie aka "Pie" and Tommy Sr. aka "Bubby"), as well as family and friends in Blytheville.

Later on in life, when I asked my Dad about his feelings during that move and the great distance it created between us, he stated how extremely difficult it was for him and my Grandma Ruth to handle, but they understood it as a needful decision made by my Mom and her new partner [Tony]. As far as Tony stepping in as a father figure, he was a natural. He was always nice and caring. I do not ever recall harboring any bad or mixed feelings toward him. He never pretentiously nor overbearingly attempted to replace my biological father – something I appreciate and love him for to this day.

Fast forward to my entering the sixth grade. I was an official resident of Blytheville, Arkansas. Life in Blytheville was entirely different than life in Chicago. The environment alone was nothing in comparison to Chicago. First and foremost, the summer temperatures were much hotter, accommodated by high humidity and mugginess that I have never experienced up until then. There were not many alleys, no houses with basements, a tremendously smaller population, and the houses and neighborhood landscapes were very much different than those in

Chicago. A plus side was the extreme friendliness of the people, always smiling and speaking – totally unlike true Chicagoans.

Although different, Blytheville was a place where freedom fun began for me. The fun provided in Blytheville consisted of swimming in the flooded streets brought on by heavy rains, playing hide and seek, and being able to explore freely outside with parents not having to worry too much about lurking troubles. The only catch was we had to be in the house before the streetlights came on.

There was one time, while we were playing in the dirt, when one of my friends told me that if I put my head close enough to the ground, I could hear the devil and his wife arguing. Being curious and trusting, I held my ear close to the ground and suddenly she pushed my head in the dirt. I didn't get too upset, it was all in fun as we as children did back then – we were tough by nature. It really didn't take long for me to make friends in Blytheville. I was always a happy-go-lucky, nice kid and made good grades.

Blytheville was where I was first introduced to church through an event called 'Street Rage.' Street Rage was like an outside church service/concert for youth. They would play worship music, and quiz us on the Bible for prizes and pizza. At that time, I did not have a clear understanding of Christ or the whole 'church' thing. Although I did love the atmosphere of Street Rage and the prizes, I cannot recall ever having a relationship with God – for me during that time, it was all about being a kid and having fun.

Speaking of Street Rage, I am reminded of another life 'lesson-learned' incident that had taken place. Unlike the Tylenol incident with my father, this one had my mom up at bat for disciplining me. I had ridden my bike to Street Rage one day and had a great time. When it was over and time for me to return home, I was so wrapped up in the excitement of what I'd just been a part of that I had forgotten I had ridden my bike and ended up walking home. My Mom was so upset when I came home without that bike. We walked back up there to double check and the bike was nowhere to be found. After that, she never bought me another bike. If she did it was a long time after that, and I simply don't recall. Far from Dad's 'butt whooping', Mom's discipline and teaching moment was, "If you lose it, you're not getting another one!" – period.

     For the most part my mom was always in my life, but there came a time when she was not. During that sorrowful period, my grandparents [Pie and Bubby] stepped in to take care of Cora, Man-Man and me, along with our youngest sister, born in 1999, Matisha [Tisha]. My Mom would pop back in from time to time, but things were different and by me being the eldest child, I was particularly being affected. I had never doubted her love for us. I just knew she had her own demons to deal with.

Chapter 4

The Weights of a Child

◇◇◇◇◇◇◇◇◇◇◇

S omewhere between the ages of 10 and 14 (the years 1998-2002), a drastic life change occurred for me when my mother and Tony succumbed to an eerie lifestyle in the streets. One would think of street life in Chicago as being more impactful and instrumental in tearing a family apart rather than a place such as small-town Blytheville; but I now know that the desires within are not confined by the outside environment. Relocating to any place doesn't change the nature within – the nurturing of inner desires will be fulfilled by any means. Out of respect for Mom and Tony, what happened and how they got to such a place is a story for them alone to tell. However, I will share my take on the ordeal and how I was personally affected.

When they chose street life, I personally did not feel that it lessened their love for me. I felt there was something much stronger and out of the ordinary that was controlling and leading them down a path of destruction. Yeah, you hear of bad things happening in the streets, at school, and on television all the time.

It is an entirely different matter when it hits home personally. I was definitely hurt, angry, and in total disbelief of how our once happy home, with Tony and Mom, had become a devastating emotional and mental nightmare due to their absence. Think about it for a split second from a child's perspective. One moment life is grand and the next moment everything has fallen apart, leaving you with unfamiliar, mixed feelings that you are not equipped to contend with as a child. As a child, it was very difficult dealing with embarrassing street gossip along with the absence of a mother who had always been nothing less than 'happy-go-lucky', supportive, and ever-present. It was earth shattering and mind-boggling for me. I believe my siblings were too young to remember and/or process the brunt of the happenings.

During the period of Mom and Tony living in the streets, my grandparents ['Bubby' and 'Pie'] had taken my siblings and me into their home. Life with my grandparents was bittersweet. I loved living with them but missed my mom terribly. Even now, mere thoughts of that moment in time gets me teary-eyed. If I recall correctly, my grandparent's house was a medium-gray colored, vinyl siding home, consisting of three bedrooms. It was one level, with my bedroom located near the front door entrance. Surprisingly, the walkway from the front porch led to the sidewalk, which was rare because to most of the areas in Blytheville did not have sidewalks. Not too distant and on the same street, there was a park [Walker's Park] with a public swimming pool as well as the home of our church pastor and his family. My grandparents ensured we attended church regularly, as they were in the process of becoming more committed than they were in Chicago – especially with all that was going on with

Mom and Tony. Although we did not see Mom much, I was happy to know she kept us in mind by checking in on us from time to time. There was this one time, out of the blue, she sent me a bag full of Tommy Hilfiger shirts. That moment gave me a sense of hope for her return soon – it was simply a child's wishful thinking.

My grandparents always took good care of us. I may not have always agreed with their methods of parenting, but I respected and knew they meant well. Besides going to church, hanging with the "preacher's kids" and being allowed to have company sometimes, I did not go many places initially. Everything was pretty much a facade to cover up the painful absence of my mom from our lives. I am not sure when my grandparents became Christians or serious about their faith but, from what I can remember, my life with them in Blytheville was completely centered around the church.

The church we attended was considered a Pentecostal 'holiness' church – meaning there were many strict rules we had to adhere to, from how we acted to dress codes [including not being allowed to wear pants]. For a preteen coming from Chicago who was used to having fun, this was an awakening experience that took time to get used to. The other pressure of being at this particular church was the requirement of being baptized. Okay, I'm a preteen going through a major personal issue in my home life; yet, the biggest concern of church leadership was for me to get baptized – something I knew nothing about at the time. What's a kid to do? The answer is, fall in line and give them what they want – after all, what did I know as a kid?

One Sunday while service was wrapping up, the pastor called out to me loudly asking, "Antoinette, when are you going to get baptized?" I was totally caught off guard and unprepared on how to answer. Hesitantly, I replied, "next week." The previous week, there were some other members in the church that had gotten baptized, so I figured I'd just do it as a way of fitting in. Also, I believe my grandparents got baptized that previous week, and that too played into my feelings of being obligated to get baptized as well. I will be the first to tell anyone, without a doubt, I was definitely not ready! How could I be ready? I was not sure if I completely understood what baptism represented, and I did not care to ask. I was feeling extremely uncomfortable with the guilt and conviction that came along with taking that big step. Anyway, the following Sunday, I went ahead and timidly got baptized – keeping my word. In keeping with the church beliefs, I went to school giving away all my pants as I began a somewhat permanent transition to dresses and skirts. I was outwardly making the transition to an appearance of what was considered "holiness."

Besides attending church, for whatever reason, moving around remained a constant with our family – whether it was with Mom or my grandparents. We lived with my grandparents in that house for about a little over a year and then moved into another house, one street over, which we stayed in for a few years. This house I remember vividly. It was tan-colored brick, one level, and had three bedrooms. We always entered through the side door from the driveway (which was the entrance to the kitchen), which led directly into the dining room, then the living room. My grandparent's bedroom was close to the side door. My siblings and I had bedrooms adjacent to one another.

At one point, my uncle, Randall [Mom's youngest brother] lived there as well. He would always sleep on the sofa in the living room. Uncle Randall was short, maybe five feet tall, and dark-complexioned. Although he was a grown-up [maybe in his late twenties/early thirties], he was a fun-loving kid at heart, who would at times walk around inside the house holding a pillow and sucking his thumb [a childhood habit he had never managed to break free from]. As weird as it may be, I was used to seeing it and thought nothing much of it. Randall was who he was, unique and fun-loving, and everyone pretty much enjoyed his company. He kept my best friend, Tameka, and I laughing quite often. Speaking of Tameka, she and I would eat chicken nuggets every time she visited our house – that was our 'go to' meal while having our usual girl talk. She would later be the person who introduced me to my first child's [son – Key'Andre aka 'Nook'] father.

Being at that house, I would oftentimes watch Grandma cook and want to learn and help. Grandma was a very good cook! I am sure she learned her cooking skills from Big Ma. There were times when Grandma would cook salmon croquettes and rice, or liver with onions, gravy and rice. It always smelled AMAZING, but for whatever reason I would not eat any of it – just being a picky eater. Instead, I'd eat a sandwich. Eating ham sandwiches after Wednesday night church services was common; however, I would still end up having to clean the dishes – something I did not particularly care for (actually despised). Sometimes I would purposely not eat anything, in hopes it would get me out of washing dishes. NEGATIVE! There were many days I fell asleep and had forgotten to clean the dishes, which resulted in me later jumping up out of my sleep to do so before my granddaddy discovered them uncleaned.

Living on the same street as I were a couple of my closest friends. There was one friend I visited almost every day and her name was Candice. She lived across the street, a few houses down. Her family always treated me as if I were their own, but, humorously, her two little brothers liked me as their girlfriend. They were both cute; nothing more than that. At times, Candice would let me borrow a pair of her blue jeans, since I had been made to give all of mine away. I sneakily wore those pants at every available opportunity. I was trying my best to subtly get back into the normality of wearing pants, although I knew that neither the church nor my grandparents were having it. Soon enough, I would develop stealth skills that would keep them from knowing anything I didn't want them to know.

Chapter 5

I Need to Know More

◇◇◇◇◇◇◇◇◇◇

I was not considered a "fast' girl during the time I had somewhat of an interest in church life; but I candidly admit, my curiosities beyond church life were starting to get the best of me. It was at that pivotal stage in life that I really wish I had my Mom to talk with and help guide me. Grandma was present, but she was wrapped up in church and spent much time being constantly worried about Mom, which left me to figure out some things on my own. Around the age of 12 or 13, I had begun looking at my appearance and body in a whole new light. I was intently embracing my figure [having a flat tummy and curves in all the right places]. As a young girl at that stage, I, like many tween girls without much guidance was very impressionable and quickly drawn to explore. There were times I would wait until my grandparents ran errands away from the house and then stand on the porch in my skirt and tube top, hoping to be seen and complimented – seeking needed attention by somebody, anybody.

Hilariously, I did get the attention of someone. It was a girl who used to pass our house, riding her bike up and down the street, constantly looking at me. For the longest of times, I thought she wanted to fight. It turned out she just wanted to be my friend – Silly me! I do not know which was worse; that incident, or the time I was hanging with this really cute boy next door. We were around the same age. He was tall, slim, caramel complexioned with light brown eyes and a low haircut. We would regularly 'chill' and talk. I was thinking we had a special chemistry, which could develop into a relationship. To my surprise one day, as we were outside talking, my little sister, Cora, came to tell me something. As she was walking back towards the house, he said to me, "She is going to be a heartbreaker when she grows up." I was purely stunned! There I was, along with him in age, strongly digging him, and thinking he liked me. All the while, it was my little sister, who was around 6 or 7 years old at the time, whom he was checking out. I figured it was because she had a lighter complexion and thought to myself, "What else could he possibly see in my younger sister, who is 6 years younger than me?" Well, I suppose this was the beginning of what sparked personal premature negative thoughts about myself which affected my self-esteem.

I loved my siblings but, like most younger siblings, they followed me around and annoyed me. At the time I was not thinking about it, but I am sure they looked up to me, no matter how imperfect I was. My baby sister, Tisha, was definitely the favorite of us children by my grandparents. Not only was she the baby of the bunch, but she was also just so cute, lovable, and always happy – so how could she not be the favorite? Being so young and far apart in age, my siblings and I never talked much or long to one another about our feelings regarding our mom being gone. However, I am willing to bet that we shared similar questions and hurtful and saddened feelings. It was definitely difficult having Mom pop in and out of our lives. She would be home for days one time; then, upon leaving, she would say she'll be back shortly and not come back for days at a time. Initially, I was really sad – I would mourn deeply in my heart! After so many times, I got to a point where I did not believe her anymore – her empty promises had deafened my ears and tortured my heart. By that time, sadly, I had become used to her routine disappointments. I knew my younger siblings did not fully understand what was going on just as I, being the elder, could not make sense of the madness. Although Mom was still with her boyfriend, Tony, I do not recall seeing much of him either.

With moving being common, it was not exclusive to changing houses only. Upon moving into that house, we also changed where we attended church. There was another Pentecostal church that sat on the corner from our house, facing a busy main street. The church was a very spacious two-story building with many offices and Sunday school rooms down the hall on the first floor. With the second floor being renovated, all services were held on the first level. Exhaustingly for us kids, we were in church at LEAST three days a week.

There were weekly choir practices, Bible studies, and our regular services on Sundays and Wednesdays. Services were long but for the most part I enjoyed them. After all, they presented opportunities for seeing and sitting with my friends there. The congregation consisted of many awesome families from different walks of life. Shamefully, some of our less fortunate members were mocked by other members for how they looked and dressed – but never by me. That was something I found very disturbing. Upon witnessing such ill-behavior, although I was closer to some than others, I began making it a point to be nice and vibe [i.e., be congenial] with everyone. The connections I had made with other youngsters at the church were natural and genuine. However, some of the sermons really scared me! Maybe it was because I was dealing with my own insecurities and demons.

Continuing with the church dress code, at school I was known for wearing skirts. My grandparents would not allow me to wear pants due to those Pentecostal 'holiness' church rules. Not only were females not allowed to wear pants, but jewelry, nail polish and other apparel were off limits as well. Females were "biblically" subjected to being all-around "plain Janes." With all of these church restrictions, my thought was "Why would anyone want to be like me?" This legalistic church life was only adding to what I was already dealing with concerning to my mom.

Chapter 6

The Search for Attention

<><><><><><><><><><><>

Although I was experiencing personal issues about my Mom, I still managed to keep my grades up and never got into any trouble at school. As a matter of fact, I developed a knack for writing poems, too. As I now think about it, I remember one of the cutest boys in school asking me to write a poem for him to give to the girl he was dating. Unbeknownst to me, somehow things got mixed-up, the girl thought I wrote that poem to her from myself. I was overly embarrassed, to say the least!

I seem to have always had a love for writing in general, whether poems, letters, etc. One time, my writing got me into so much trouble. I was in either the 7th or 8th grade and for whatever reason, I had foolishly written a really explicit poem. I knew nothing about sex and was a virgin, but I somehow knew enough to put in writing some adult sexually laced words that would make a sailor blush. Writing something like that at an early age, I can now only imagine how the demons must have been swarming around like buzzards and working even harder to initiate me into the devil's army. Anyhow, I was proud of what I had written and decided to share it with all of my friends and associates because I thought it was really good – an interesting rhyme with a nice flow.

Due to my negligence and being super excited, it was shared and put into the wrong hands. Someone, not sure who, gave it to the teacher, and the school contacted my grandparents. I knew I was in some hot water that I could not get out of! I do not specifically recall what my punishment was, but listening to my grandparents reading it aloud was undeniably punishment enough. It seems my acting out and curiosity were starting to worsen – the effects of personal issues and stresses were subtly and surely beginning to manifest rapidly.

Soon after that incident, I was riding the school bus one day, and the guy I had a crush on asked if I wanted to have sex. Although it had temptingly crossed my mind, there was a stronger thought of it being a most disgusting thing to do. So, I turned him down for that invitation. However, it sparked the beginning of me becoming a "kissing bandit". Even though I turned that guy down for sex, I would "slob him down" [French kiss] in the hallway during bathroom breaks while in school. Next thing I knew, after so many occurrences, I had soon become an addicted kissing machine. There were two guys I always kissed when I saw them in the hallway. I would ask for a bathroom pass just so I could walk to the bathroom in hopes that one of them would be there. We would share passionate kisses and head back to our classes like nothing happened. Speaking honestly, there's nothing like tasting sin that makes you feel so good, especially when you are going through things emotionally, personally, and spiritually – it all made great soil for the devil to execute his plans of destruction.

Besides kissing boys in the school's hallways, cheerleading served as a recreational outlet for me. Although I was not the most flexible person, could not do proper backflips, nor do a split, I really enjoyed being a cheerleader. Like most things in my life, it was not easy. My time as a cheerleader was far from what you would imagine. We were not a group of popular girls hanging out with the football players and eating lunch together. In fact, it was the complete opposite. I did not like or look at any of the football players as 'got to have hunks' and I mostly hung out with a group of girls who were just as wonderful and unpopular as I was.

As much as I enjoyed cheerleading, there was one incident that haunted me for a long time – the day I got tackled while cheering on the football field. That night was like any other, the bleachers were full, and we were on the field and excited to cheer for our team football players. As the boys were running their play, they headed straight towards where we [cheerleaders] were. I must have been zoned out because I did not see them coming, nor do I recall anyone yelling at me to move out of the way. They tackled me so fast and with such brute force that it lifted me in the air and I almost hit the gate on my way to the ground. Surprisingly, I was not hurt at all or maybe I was, and the pain was suppressed due to the embarrassment. I did not realize it at the time, but I must have been a physically strong young lady. From that point forward, everytime the football players would see me, they would bring up that night and laugh in my face – a very pathetic thing to do. They may have done it in the name of 'fun-and-games', but it was so annoying hearing that EVERY SINGLE DAY and it was a self-esteem killer, too. Thank God I did not let it bring me to the point of suicidal thoughts at that time.

Looking back, I am very thankful for the measure of faith and God's strength that I needed to get through personal pains, hurts, and hang-ups. Although the church could be out of touch or filled too much with negativity, it did provide me with a glimpse of the presence of God! Soon after that incident, things had finally died down and, boy, was I grateful – because the summer before high school was about to bring with it way more unimaginable troubles.

Chapter 7

Hormonal Upstart

◇◇◇◇◇◇◇◇◇

T here was a turning point on the horizon for me at the age of 14. Turning points can be deemed as either bad or good. For me, I would just say for the most part they were learning experiences along with a tragic incident that took God's grace, protection, and healing for me to understand and grow beyond those wounds. Naively, here in America, many possess a generalized "hakuna matata" [i.e., there is no trouble] idea that teenagers should be doing "innocent teenage" things such as playing board games and hanging with friends. Truth be told, those "innocent teenage" things encompass much more than adults know of and rarely acknowledge. That is, teenagers have restless minds that hunger for new information and experiences – they need to be fed constantly. However, what they feed on is where the success and/or problem lies.

I would strongly argue that the mind of a teenager is intuitively inquisitive and prone to testing boundaries. Come on! Think back to your teenage years. Did you not test the boundaries of those "no's" or "because I said so's" that were sternly stated by adults to prevent you from doing or getting something that you may have found to be somewhat enticing? No matter how strong any teenager may think they are, given the right target, timing, and opportunity, temptation will prevail through our actions roughly 99.9% of the time. Once the temptation is tasted and sin has a foothold, as the old adage goes, "It costs us more than we can afford to pay and keeps us longer than we intend to stay."

Although I was a virgin and knew it to be honorable, at the age of 14, I begin having strong urges to forego what I was told and taught in exchange for fulfilling my desires. With my grandparents strictly forbidding me from having a boyfriend, I took it as a dare. The setup and opportunity to do so couldn't have been more perfect or let's just say that the devil knows how to set the scene for temptation. There was this young man whom I liked very much and with whom I was frequently having engaging conversations. He was tall and stocky with a dark complexion. I thought highly of him, mainly because he was a local rapper on the grind [focused and about his business]. We would share lengthy conversations on the phone just about every night. I had my own cell phone and my minutes were free after 9:00 pm. He was the guy who I just KNEW I wanted to be the first and only person to whom I lost my virginity. Whenever we talked, I would be sure to make it known to him. The ridiculousness about it was that we were not in a relationship – just good friends. Temptation along with my determination overruled all sense of reality, morality, and consequences. Quite frankly, the teenage hormones were fully kicking into high gear.

I was aware of him talking, flirting, and most likely having sex with other girls but none of that bothered nor deterred me. I would write love letters to him, doodle his name on my notebooks, and just melt whenever he walked past me in the school hallways. One day as I was doodling his name in one of my notebooks, this girl approached and asked, "Are you talking to him?" Boldly, I replied, "Yes!" Brazenly, she responded, "Me too!" On a side note, ironically, I think that may have been the predecessor of the "me too" movement we all witness in this day and age. Anyway, his pursuing and talking to us both did not matter to neither her nor me. He would come to my locker to get a letter from me, go to the other girl's locker and get a letter from her, and then he would proceed to his 'official' girlfriend's locker to walk with her to class. Yes, he was a true "player" who had it like that. The "official" girlfriend never said anything to me, but her friend had no love at all for the other girl and me! I had no doubt she literally hated me – strong words, but that is the truth. She [his 'official' girlfriend's friend] would bully me every time she saw me in the hallway. Because of my infatuated feelings for him, I uneasily endured the bullying and fact of her disliking me. Little did I know, this wishful romance would soon come to a crashing end when I met his cousin a short time later.

Chapter 8

Manipulated Innocence

◇◇◇◇◇◇◇◇◇◇◇

It was 2002, the summer before high school, where it all began. Being the social butterfly I was [and still am], I was never one for being planted indoors. I enjoy being on the go, in the know, and ready to grow. Along with each passing year came the anticipation of freedom which led to me getting out of the house a little more and meeting new people. Could it have been that I was missing and needed my parents? Or, could it have been that I was needing an escape to suppress the subtle pain and disappointments coupled with strict church rules that did nothing for my emotional state of being? I can't say for sure, but it just felt good to be ANYWHERE ELSE besides church, school, or home.

During that summer, my cousin Tasha and I would often go walking, which was a popular thing to do in Blytheville. Everyone loved to walk or post-up [i.e. loiter] in certain neighborhoods just to talk, hangout and be seen. If I wasn't walking, I was riding in cars with some of my friends from church. One clear sunshiny hot and beautiful day while walking, I laid eyes on one of the sexiest young men I had ever seen, at least at that time in my life. He was talking and posted with a group of friends. I distinctly remember him as being tall, dark complexioned, and wearing gray shorts that complemented his stunning bowlegs. I was wearing a blue jean skirt and one of the Tommy Hilfiger shirts my Mom had given me. As we were walking, he brashly made his way over to Tasha and me and began making small talk with us. I believe he either sensed my attraction to him or he noticed me drooling [Lol!]. After a short conversation and without hesitation, he and I exchanged phone numbers and began a "friendship" [so I thought].

Throughout those summer outings, I was able to meet a lot of guys. The routine was I and them exchanging phone numbers, talking on the phone, and hanging out at their favorite spots – nothing more. It was my way of developing a 'supposed' friendship in which I was valued. With the steady phone calls and compliments, they would make me feel very good about myself. Even the look on their faces when they saw me out and about was priceless. In hindsight, I was too naïve and immature to know they were priming me as prey. They were cunningly answering the call of my shallow self-esteem with words and acts of affirmation; slowly warming me up in preparation for having me as a 'meal' later. Although my family would say kind and supportive words to and about me, it was not the same as receiving those words from the males I met outside. I'll be the first to admit, it is very important for a girl to have the guy she admires the most in the home – her father. I firmly believe that if my Mom and father had stayed together with all of us living under one roof, the chances of my experiencing heartaches would have been decreased dramatically. That statement is not meant to displace 100 percent blame on my parents for what was about to happen, but their absence did fuel part of the reason of my wandering astray.

My friendliness with males was never intended to open the door to promiscuity, but all of those immoral thoughts did entice my flesh and bring happiness to me quite often. Receiving all the newfound attention made for a creative mind in this teenage gal! Having accumulated a plethora of prospects, the thought of wanting the guy [local rapper] whom I was crazy about to be my first was slowly dissipating from my mind.

Like I've stated before and will say again, given the elements of right timing, target, and opportunity, what you thought you wouldn't do to fulfill an urge, you will find yourself doing. As chance would have it, those elements were aligned perfectly for me in regard to losing my sexual innocence. The day I lost my virginity is a time that I will never forget. There was this guy who lived on the same street as I did. He was medium-brown complexioned with a nice smile and a low haircut. I had known him for a while as he would seemingly always flirt everytime I went walking in the neighborhood. Many times, I would intentionally walk near where he lived, hoping he was outside. I liked the attention but never had any sexual thoughts about him during our initial conversations interactions.

One pleasant, warm summer day in 2002, while a lingering curiosity about having sex had overtaken all my senses, I and a friend girl were having a talk about sex. During the discussion, I informed her of my plan to lose my virginity to this guy I really liked and met earlier in the day; however, it would require her staying the night with me at my grandparent's house. She was a couple of years younger than I and very impressionable, which played in my favor. She was eager to go along with the plan and thought of it as a "cool" thing to do.

Sadly, the same gimmick the guys were playing on me, I unconsciously adapted and put into practice against my grandparents by manipulating their trust in me. They loved me dearly, but were oblivious to my deceitfulness and shenanigans. I went about the day buttering up my grandparents by making sure chores were done and anything they asked or needed was taken care of – which I did happily. They agreed to allow my friend girl to stay over that night; and, I couldn't have been happier. My friend and I spent most of our time in my bedroom, anxiously waiting for night to befall and my grandparents and siblings to fall asleep. As anticipated, a few hours had passed by seemingly like seconds within a minute. The daylight quickly faded into darkness and the night was finally upon us, hinting it was now time to put phase one of the plan into action by sneaking out of the house.

I slowly and carefully crept through the house to peek inside my grandparents' and sibling's bedrooms to make sure they were all asleep before the adventure began. Once the surveillance was completed and they were all found sound asleep, we made our way out of my bedroom window. Upon exiting the house, we hurriedly walked 3-5 miles across town to hang with these guys we had met earlier that summer. I cannot speak for her, but I was like super nervous during that walk! For some reason or another, the street traffic seemed extra busy that particular night. Such busyness only compounded my fearful thoughts of the cops stopping us for being out after curfew. Silly me, worried about being caught by the police for a curfew violation rather than the detrimental life-altering situation I was walking into.

Upon arriving we noticed the group of guys we'd met earlier sitting outside the house of the one guy's parents that I liked. As we approached them, there wasn't much said other than a simple "hello" and very little small talk ("yada yada"), just to break the ice. Besides, we all knew what we came there for [getting busy sexually]; so why waste time? Not completely sure but I guess my guy's mom was in the house because he never invited us to go in. It really didn't matter anyway. All I needed was for my "appetite" to be satisfied quickly.

Foolishly, I was trapped by the gravity of my hormones, leading me into what I thought would be a gratifying experience. It's not so much that I didn't value my innocence because, quite frankly, I hadn't given any thought to it. I was just completely headstrong with a boosted self-esteem and riding cloud 9, brought on by the mounds of attention I was receiving from so many guys. For a 14-year-old, the thought was "live and experience it all, have 'fun' and be free, by any means necessary." That thinking led to me wanting to experience the sexual intimacy part in hopes of having that "blissful high" feeling that I was yearning for.

Not ever going into the house and having very little time remaining before having to make my way back home, we had to make do with what we had. His mother had a gray minivan with three row seats parked in the yard. That minivan served as our make-shift bed. We climbed into the backseat of his mom's minivan and 'did the do'. Sure enough, I was NOT feeling it like I thought I would. It turned out to be far from how I had imagined having sex to be – especially for it being my first time. I liked him before it all happened, but in that very moment, I regretted the situation and resented him. To make matters worse, before we even had a chance to finish, he looked at me and asked if his friend can "get some," too? I had never felt so humiliated, cheap, and worthless before that instant. There I was, 14 years old, having sex for the very first time with a guy who I thought I liked, and he had the nerve to ask me can his friend "get some?" I can only assume he thought I lied about being a virgin. I firmly declined the disgusting request, got dressed, and my friend and I headed back home. As traumatic as that night was, it still was just the beginning of my troubling promiscuous life.

Chapter 9

I Didn't Know

◇◇◇◇◇◇◇

The very next day following that awfully disgusting experience, I was back to my normal routine - cooped up in the house and waiting for 9:00 pm to strike so I could talk on the phone [remember free minutes after 9pm]. That night I was on a three-way call with my neighbor across the street and that sexy, chocolate bowlegged guy who I exchanged numbers with earlier that summer. I recall telling them the entire ordeal that transpired the previous night. Although it was a traumatic situation, we light-heartedly laughed about it. For me the conversation and laughter helped to subside my real feelings. At one point, they seemed confused about why I was sharing the egregious information with them, but nonchalantly they quickly brushed it off and continued in conversation. At the end of the conversation, I senselessly invited bowlegged "Sexual-chocolate" over to my house that night. What was I thinking? Better yet, let me answer

– I wasn't thinking! As bad as the night before was, my feelings had become numb, which led to me not thinking twice about inviting him over.

That very night, upon quietly sneaking him into my bedroom via the window, as he and I were lying in my bed, he accidentally kicked the wall. Carelessly, I did not bother checking whether or not my grandparents were asleep before he came over; so, I quickly rushed toward the living room to tell my granddaddy that was an "accident" before he was able to come investigate what was going on in my bedroom. It worked like a charm as he stayed in the living room. After having intercourse and him departing through the window, I noticed I had been bleeding. I had no idea what was happening! After cleaning things up, I called to tell him about the blood. He made light humor of it, saying it was the size of his "junk." Still intrigued about why I had bled, after hanging up from talking with him, I then called and discussed the issue with other friends. They explained that it meant "he popped my cherry." At that time, I had never heard of that term. Keep in mind, no one had told me about sex.

I learned the little I knew about sex from my friends who were already sexually active and from sneakily watching "R" and "X" rated shows at night when I was younger. The most I was actually taught about sex was "not to do it until marriage" because it was a sin. Attending church on Wednesday nights were truly uncomfortable struggles. I "loved" the Lord and knew it was wrong to have sex; however, I couldn't wait until church was over so I could invite someone over on those Wednesday nights. Before I knew it, I had been with roughly eight guys in one summer. Sorrowfully, sex had become my habitual relief outlet for the unworthiness I was feeling inside. The bold and rebellious me continued on a landslide, by being intimate with several guys, night after night, and using protection was never a concern of mine. I acted as if I couldn't get pregnant. As far as contracting STD's, I wasn't concerned because, to me, they didn't exist – until they did. I contracted [curable] STD's on several occasions; but it still wasn't enough to slow me down. Absurdly, I kept going back to the same guys, not knowing or caring who gave it to me. Word about my promiscuous ways must have gotten around town because every "sexcapade" relationship I was in ended badly or led me into situations I didn't desire nor need to be in.

Chapter 10

Traumatized & Alone

◇◇◇◇◇◇◇◇◇◇

With my grandparents being strict and super religious, I wasn't allowed to go to any parties. I didn't care to party anyway, but I did enjoy being around kids my age outside of the church. However, there was one particular time I was invited to a party by yet another guy to whom I was talking. It was early summer on a school night near the end of the school year in 2002. He told me there were several girls from school who were going to be there and even offered to have some of his friends come and get me. Although I didn't have anything new or very nice to wear, I was super excited to be invited to what I expected to be a great party with friends. Early that evening, I hastily put on my favorite blue jean skirt. It was fitted, long and had what looked like bullet holes around the bottom portion. My top was a golden-colored turtleneck. With my bedroom located in the rear of the house and having the window located near the air condition unit, it was easy for me to sneak out once the guys arrived in their car near my grandparents' house.

Once I got inside the car and we were en route to the "party," the guys in the backseat were trying to feel all over my body. It was at that moment when I realized I had been placed into a bad situation. Although I had been intimate with several guys before, I never presented myself in a way that made people think I would sleep with any and everybody. For me, there was an inkling of a relationship developed over time with the guys before; I, at least, formed some type of friendship and actually LIKED the guys, some I even felt like I loved.

Upon arriving at the house, where the supposed party was to be, I saw that none of the females he named were there. It was a house full of guys, with each of them being either 18 or 19 years of age, and there I was the lone 14-year-old female. In hindsight, I should have asked to be taken home right then and there; instead, I walked into his bedroom and sat on the bed alone. Shortly after, some other guy came in and started undressing himself. NO, this was NOT the guy who invited me! It was one of his friends. Petrified, I didn't know what to do or say – I was definitely in a state of shock. Without question nor hesitation, he proceeded to have sex with me. Next thing I knew, the other guys were following suit, one by one, picking up where the other left off. I distinctly remember seeing nothing more than a bright light, like a flashlight or cell phone. I cannot say with surety how many guys were in the room nor do I quite remember who was being intimate with me versus who was just there watching.

During and especially after this painfully heart-wrenching ordeal, I felt extremely dirty, terrible, and so used. In the midst of it all happening, I never said "NO." Therefore, they never stopped, until they were finished with me – like a piece of trash. The last person who took in on the action was the guy I really liked. He too did what he wanted with me and then pretended to be sleep when I asked him to take me home. Thankfully, one of the other guys who was still there took me home. I don't think this guy was in the room when everything transpired, but then again, I don't know because I was so out of touch with reality. It was like having an out of body experience – or should I say NIGHTMARE! The guy who had driven me home seemingly had a demeanor of sorrowfulness for me and what I had just endured.

This situation happened near the end of the school year and on a school night. The next day, somehow the entire school knew the rumored version of what went down. Without any show of remorse or compassion for me, everyone had chosen to gossip about it instead. It was very humiliating, with the worst part being the fact that no one actually knew or wanted the truth! They just talked about it as if I willingly allowed all of these guys to "run a train" on me. I've never been the type to like or cause confrontation, so I didn't clear things up and allowed them to believe and gossip as they wished. At that time, the last thing I wanted to do was cry "rape," because I felt that I technically didn't say "No" or "Stop," which meant I was somewhat or silently consenting. Not sure which was worse, that day or the day I got drunk soon after that incident for the first time ever.

For you readers, before you judge, remember that I was a 14-year-old dealing with physical, emotional, mental, and parental issues – I was incapable of exercising more mature judgement with a sound mind. What happened to me is something that should never have happened to anyone. Back then I felt meaningless in the eyes of many and voiceless against the harms and dangers I prematurely walked into. Now that I am older and definitely wiser with God, I know my worth and will use my voice to the fullest extent possible helping pull others up, out, and away from circumstances that are created to kill their spirits, steal their innocence, and destroy their purpose. God takes our brokenness to rebuild a powerful testimony for saving others.

Chapter 11

Exacerbated Troubles

◇◇◇◇◇◇◇◇◇◇◇

As the summer weeks of 2002 were coming to a close, I found myself talking to the local rapper (the guy I'd mentioned earlier about wanting to lose my virginity to), whom I considered being my "first love." Like all the previous guys, he was nice and a great conversationalist – knowing all the right words to say that satisfied what I wanted to hear. You would think I should have learned the game by then and avoided these types of guys. However, with my self-esteem being at an all-time low, I found myself gravitating toward these types of characters and accepting those relationships as normal.

One day as he and I were riding in his car and drinking alcohol, he took me to a location where some of his friends were. If this scenario sounds familiar, it's because it was just as the last incident was, but included the use of alcohol and there being three guys there that night. With the last incident happening weeks ago, I figured there was no way for it to happen again. I was so wrong! Having drank some Hennessey and coca cola (not even a lot – I was a lightweight so it didn't take much for me to become intoxicated), things began to appear blurry. I am unable to descriptively recount all that had taken place. The only clear memory I have is the guy carrying me back to the car because I was too intoxicated to walk. Unlike what happened before, this situation was never passed through the gossip mill nor brought up again by any of the guys nor me. Although my relationship and conversation with each male partner was at different levels, I never felt like I couldn't trust them until I was put in a situation where that trust was lost.

After months – yes, months – of not getting pregnant, I met my soon to be "baby's daddy." I met him through an old friend at a high school football game. It was kind of like a blind date. He seemed very different than the guys I previously "dated." By that time, I had developed a fixed attraction to "bad boys" who gave me thug-life vibes. Surprisingly, that was not the character of this guy. He was super sweet and didn't come off as a pretentious bad boy at all. He really wasn't my type of guy, but strangely, I liked that about him. We talked for a little while and quickly made plans to meet up for sex later that evening. Honestly, I really didn't want to, but sex had become a staple of my nature. I liked his swag because he seemed like a "good boy," and I really wasn't "feeling" him enough to have sex with him – but I did. We had sex one time and after that I was back to hooking up with the guys I was talking to on the regular.

I never really feared getting pregnant because I had experienced way too many unprotected encounters and it never happened. I considered myself invulnerable. Guess what? I was wrong. I remember the day I found out I was pregnant. I was in the bathroom vomiting what looked like egg yolk and totally afraid to tell and disappoint my grandparents. They were deep into church, and I KNEW it was going to be a big deal with them and the church leadership. Besides, I was living the typical story of a "church girl" hypocrite. In church all week, singing in the choir, and out fornicating at every opportunity. Anyway, what was also troubling is not knowing who the father was. How was I to tell my grandparents that I was pregnant AND didn't know who the father was? Somehow, I managed to hide it from my grandparents for almost eight months.

I remember being at my second cousin, Tasha's house, laying on her bed. Her mom [my first cousin] asked me point blank, "Are you pregnant?" I sat up quickly and said, "NO!" She intuitively knew better and tried to tell my grandparents several times but I denied it every single time. I got angry and questioned, "Why is she in my business?" The whole time I was trying to figure out how to tell them [my grandparents] I was pregnant. We had never talked about pregnancy or sex - EVER!

At school my friends were surprised that my grandparents didn't know because I was almost eight months pregnant and showing! I then remember being in school during 7th period class and telling my classmates this was the day I was going to tell my grandparents. Upon making that decision, I was super nervous for the rest of the school day and could barely focus. In my heart, I knew that my grandparents would never kick me out but a small thought in my mind made me feel like they would.

Upon school being dismissed for the day, I got on the bus as usual and headed home carrying a heavy burden of guilt and shame. Once I got off the bus and walked through the door of my grandparent's house, with a serious tone in her voice, my Grandma immediately called me over to the couch where she and my Grandpa were sitting. She asked, "Antoinette, are you pregnant?" Instantaneously, I started crying and confessed. Their next question was, "Who is the father?", as if they would know if I told them. I named the guy who I thought it may have been, which was the last guy I slept with. They were disappointed but obviously didn't kick me out of the house. They made me call and tell my Dad and grandma Ruth in Chicago, my Mom when she called from prison, and the pastor at the church we attended.

My family was very disappointed but, weirdly, I felt the worst part was having to tell the pastor. I was questioning within, "Why did I have to tell the pastor?" After all, he wasn't family and I'd figured he and his family had already known because I went to school with their son and others from the church who were 'in the know' through gossip. When the pastor and 'company' learned that I was pregnant, they were also told about me having rubella, thanks to my grandparents. It was there in the pastor's office, that he and his wife along with my grandparents and a few other church members, began praying for me. Although they may not have meant any harm, in that moment, I felt like they were praying for me as if I were the devil himself. With everyone openly knowing, it made for a worse church experience. For instance, during Sunday school, the pastor's son would try to shame me with snide remarks about me being pregnant. Fortunately, there were two girls in Sunday school who I considered my sisters, who always took up for me and redirected his conversations. I don't think the Sunday school teacher ever caught on. Being pregnant at 14 with a background of promiscuity was one thing, but having to go through this pregnancy at a Pentecostal church was a whole different ball game! I needed my Mom home more than ever.

Chapter 12

My Son

◇◇◇◇

My time of being pregnant didn't pose much of a health challenge for me. My pre-pregnancy weight was around 120 pounds. My maximum pregnancy weight was 160 pounds. My post-pregnancy weight was 124 pounds on average. Throughout the pregnancy, my cravings were for chili dogs – not ice cream and/or pickles, just chili dogs. I did not experience any health complications during the entire pregnancy. As a matter of fact, I had not received any prenatal care until a little after eight months because I was attempting to keep the pregnancy hidden from my family as long as possible. Up until the actual delivery date, I was continually on the go; never one for sitting down because it only bored me.

Upon passing the purported due date, it was determined that my son would be a late arrival. The doctor allowed a couple of days before deciding to induce delivery. During the evening of Tuesday, August 12, 2003, I was having this very uncomfortable feeling. I was not having any pain, just felt totally uncomfortable. I figured I just needed to find a relaxed position to rest. Around 4:00 am on Wednesday, I experienced my water breaking. I calmly got up, dressed myself in a blue jean skirt and t-shirt, and awakened my mom [who'd recently moved in with us] and grandparents to take me to the hospital. We rushed to awaken and get my younger siblings ready and were on our way, dashing out the house. As we got into the vehicle, I put a towel between my legs, and we hurriedly headed to the hospital.

Luckily, the hospital was roughly five minutes away. As we arrived at the hospital, the contractions were beginning to be very painful! I was rushed into the emergency room, placed on a gurney, wheeled to a delivery room, and put under close observation in preparation for giving birth. I was dilating regularly, then suddenly hit a plateau at about seven and a half centimeters. I was then told I had to have a Caesarean section [aka C-section]. I don't recall being thoroughly informed about vaginal birth vs C-section until that very moment in the delivery room. Keep in mind, I was a 14-year-old whose first pregnancy appointment did not occur until I was about eight months pregnant! Preparing for the C-section called for me to get an epidural, which is an anesthesia injected in your spinal cord that numbs the pain. The doctor administering the epidural injection specifically told me not to jump or I could be paralyzed! Between my nerves and that freezing delivery room, I was unable to stop flinching. Thank God I didn't get paralyzed because I definitely jumped as soon as that needle entered my spine!

As the epidural was kicking in, I recall fading in and out and feeling like I couldn't breathe, even with the oxygen mask on. The medical staff kept reassuring me that I was fine, which I was, but that feeling was definitely legit. Wednesday, August 13,

2003, was the beginning of a beautiful new chapter in my life. Around noon, I had finally given birth to a very healthy son, Key'Andre, weighing eight pounds and 12 ounces. He had a light complexion, large-sized lips, curly black hair, and green eyes. I don't remember seeing him immediately upon giving birth because of being heavily medicated, but my mom always reminds me of her thoughts being, "Well, that's my baby", when she first saw him. She was implying that he wasn't that cute, but we would love him anyway. By the time I was able to see him clearly, he had been cleaned, a little less swollen, and super cute – even though my mom's humorous statement still makes me laugh every time I think about it.

After giving birth, my health was crucially in question. I had developed a high fever, which required me to stay in the hospital for an entire week. Oftentimes, I cried out of loneliness and being away from home for what I considered to be an extended length of time. All I could think about was getting better and finding a way to adjust to being a mother. Was God in my thoughts? Truthfully, not really. At the time, I felt I was dealing with real-world situations that required me being with my family rather than seeking after something or someone that was not tangible. In hindsight, I see God's mercy on this child, primarily because of my praying grandparents.

Chapter 13

Daddy?

◇◇◇◇

A most memorable moment, during that week's stay in the hospital, was a visitation by the guy who I THOUGHT was Key'Andre's father, along with his disgruntled girlfriend. He was tall, light complexioned, stocky, and had green eyes. He held Key'Andre and stayed for a few minutes, but not too long, because his girlfriend was upsettingly pacing in and out of the room and rushing him to leave. He was very impassive as he held Key'Andre for about a minute while playing with his hands for a few seconds. There was little to no conversation between he and I; his girlfriend made sure of that. Personally, I cannot say it mattered much – it was what it was just as I was who I was [young, naïve, and seeking love and acceptance through faulty experiences].

As the time had come for me to leave the hospital and go home, my emotions were at an all-time high. Although I was happy to go home and happy to have a healthy baby, I dreaded the anticipated events that would follow once I got back to reality.

I gave birth to my son the very month [August] school started, which delayed my official school start date by six weeks [late September]. During those six weeks, it was well-coordinated for me to get my schoolwork sent home, completed, and returned so I could stay on track. When the time came for me to return to school in-person, it was bittersweet. I missed my friends, but I knew that I would get hounded with questions and receive unwelcoming negative attitudes, looks, and treatment.

Other than the minor contentions at school, life was going smoothly. The operative word is "WAS." Issues outside of school arose regarding the legitimacy of my son's biological father. As previously stated, my son was born light complexioned with green eyes, just like the guy who visited the hospital, held him, and who I THOUGHT was his father. Even if he was the father, he was not owning up to the responsibilities of being a father nor providing any type of support. However, as my son was getting older, his looks began to drastically change. My friend, Tameka, observed his looks changing and told me that was her cousin's baby. He was the guy I was setup with at the game the previous summer. In my heart I knew he was the father from the moment I noticed my son's lips when he was around six months old. Nonetheless, I was hoping it wasn't his child because I didn't want to go through any more drama with him. Besides, my grandparents only knew of me being with one guy, so I didn't want them finding out otherwise.

During the first few years of my son's life, many of the guys I had slept with would come by to "visit." They acted concerned but in reality, they just wanted to see if my son was possibly theirs, based on any physical resemblances or specific characteristics. Hesitantly, I'd finally made up my mind to resolve this questionable issue by having a paternity test completed when my son was at the age of 3 or 4. The results came back and the guy I originally named [i.e., hospital visitor] was NOT the father. I was extremely embarrassed and somewhat disappointed.

To add further to my humiliation, I now had to come clean by telling my grandparents and really, everyone else – because by that time, nearly the entire town was gossiping about my business – when I had only shared it personally with a select few. I was very nervous having to inform my grandparents. It meant I had to tell them that I'd been with more guys than they were aware of. As I proceeded relaying the information to them, they appeared a bit shocked and confused but they remained supportive and committed to us getting through this situation.

You want to talk about someone really in need of a compassionate shoulder? That someone was definitely me! As God would have it and in His timing, I remember sitting in class and the hospital visiting guy's [the one I originally though was the father] cousin sat behind me. I guess she somehow discerned my distressed demeanor and God knew what this child [i.e., me] needed because she quietly whispered a few comforting words that everything was going to be okay. The spirit behind her words made me feel so much better at a time when I was feeling so low.

The most difficult part of being shamed had begun subsiding as it was now time for healing and dealing with the backlash. What made the backlash so awful was being in a small town where everyone knew everyone and gossip was easily spread about someone else's business. But it was that shame and backlash that pushed me closer to God. After everything that had occurred and everything I'd endured, I made a vow to God as well

as myself that I was DONE with sex – at least for the time being!
That was a vow I kept for about two years.

Chapter 14

Let's Grow

<><><><><><>

L ife as a teen mom was difficult, but thankfully I had help. I still lived with my grandparents, mom, and siblings under one roof. There were times when my mom was getting up throughout the night tending to the cries of my son while I slept for school – something I'll never forget and for which I'm forever grateful. I guess it was a mixture of her feeling remorse about me and her motherly instincts. Ironically, although she was being helpful, neither of us realized how much of her doing was actually hindering my growth as a parent.

Upon her realizing that I wasn't learning much about parenting, she wisely stopped enabling what had become my bad habit of neglect; this forced me to do better as a hands-on parent. Not that I was an awful parent, but she knew it was past time I experience those sleepless nights as a crucial part of learning and growing in parental responsibilities. I was young but I'd learned to take great care of my son through nurturing and bonding with him. Each month brought a new learning experience and a chance to put the past mentality about life behind me. After all, my future as well as my son's had become more important than anything I'd ever imagined at that point.

Church life was very interesting for this teen mom. Although there were members of the church where I attended who thought my son was cute, there were also others who appeared to be afraid to get close to either of us. They were afraid the younger children would think it was "alright" to be a teen mom and they did not want to appear as though they condoned or promoted a syndrome of teen moms. Knowing what I now know [and wish they had known], sin was committed while making the baby, but not by being the mother of a baby. They were so focused on me and my imperfect journey that they didn't realize that others in the church were discreetly going down the same path. In spite of everything that was going on, I still had no desire to belittle, mistreat, or delve into other people's business by gossiping or pointing the finger. God was at work with your girl!

Chapter 15

Attempting to Escape the Past

◇◇◇◇◇◇◇◇◇◇◇◇◇◇◇◇

Just as God was at work getting my attention, so was the devil and my flesh. The streak of not having sex came to an end at about two years after my vow to God and myself. Before I knew it, I was back to old habits. Although things weren't as extreme as before, I was definitely far from being an angel. I did manage to stay loyal to the individual relationships I was in. Although, I still wasn't allowed to have a boyfriend, my grandparents had become a tad bit more lenient. At some point, they eventually allowed me to start back wearing pants to school. Yet, the constant moving was unchanging. Prior to my 18th birthday, we had moved and were living in a different house. This was a house my grandparents had decided to purchase (which meant a strong possibility for stability). It was a one-level, three-bedroom, brick house that was located down the street from my job – my very first job – McDonald's. I was starting to get my life together for myself as well as my son.

While my grandparents always meant well, there were times they would say things that had me question what they truly thought of me. One particular time occurred when a friend of mine along with her cousin stopped by to visit me at the house. What triggered my grandparents' concern was her cousin being a male. I had departed with them with plans of spending the night at my friend's house. Realizing I had forgotten to take clothes with me, we quickly returned to my grandparents' house. As I entered the house, I was met with an argument by my grandparents insisting that I intentionally left my bedroom door open in order to bring her cousin into my bedroom. I was totally shocked and caught off-guard! I mean, what did they think I was about to do? I know my history wasn't the best, but I was never openly disrespectful nor was it in my mind to be.

Another incident that had me scratching my head happened when I came home from being with a friend. As I walked through the door, my grandfather referred to me as a "street walker", which I interpreted in my mind as "prostitute." I'm sure he didn't think I was a prostitute or anything similar, but the fact that he said that made me so upset. I quickly forgave him, but also knew that wouldn't be his last time with such snide remarks. Mixed feelings of distrust were beginning to manifest, and I knew I was partly to blame. BUT I also knew that the company they kept from the church was feeding into their views of me. The one thing I didn't do that I wish we had all done was hold open communication among ourselves as a family rather than interacting with one another based on assumptions. Unfortunately, within our community and upbringing, assumption was the routine guide, which resulted in one-sided communication, fussing, cussing, and arguments. It's very difficult to effectively and compassionately communicate when it has never been observed and/or taught to you.

My grandparents' distrust and snide remarks certainly did not help my mental state nor deter my fleshly desires. However, it did help me to begin understanding why church leaves a bad taste in the mouths of many people. People [including myself] go and learn, but rarely does it translate to them having a matured lifestyle change or better yet, a real relationship with God that shows in how we treat others. Not having that personal relationship with God left me unguarded and open for continued mischiefs.

At about 18 years of age, I had experienced my second pregnancy scare. I had met and was pursuing a relationship with this guy who was short with a medium-brown complexion, gold teeth, and a low faded haircut. Yes, we were also engaging in sex. He NEVER wanted to use protection, and he was MARRIED! I'd always suggested he use protection but never enforced it. His preference trumped my self-care. By doing things his way, there was one month my cycle didn't happen on time. I was so scared and praying desperately in secret not to be pregnant by this guy! Suddenly, at the last day of the month, I had my cycle and boy, was I glad! That scare didn't seem to stop either of us because we were back to our shenanigans soon after my cycle. You may ask, 'Why would you keep going in that direction after experiencing mercy?" My answer is, "Easy! Because I didn't have a committed relationship with God that would have changed my life." However, I would keep each show of His mercy in the pockets of my heart and mind for such a time as this – to share with others.

Going back to this same guy, he was someone I'd met one day while walking. We chopped it up [i.e., engaged in small talk] and exchanged phone numbers. I will honestly admit that I didn't know he was married at that time until I asked various people about him…and to this day, I still don't know if he was actually married when we first met or got married soon after. Either way, it was wrong, and I knew it but still proceeded being involved with him. This went on for about a year. Once his wife started to find text messages and pictures on his phone, with a firm mind, I had to end that relationship immediately. That was drama I did not want in my life. As I matured, I'd come to realize that relationship should have never existed for several shameful reasons.

Chapter 16

Danger Ahead, Beware!

◇◇◇◇◇◇◇◇◇◇◇

My son was almost three years old when I graduated May of 2006. By this time, I had a pretty good routine with my school life, church life and home life. I still had help from my grandparents and my mom, but I held it down pretty good by myself as well. The backlash and rumors had died down and I was finally in a good place in life. Things weren't perfect but I wasn't where I started.

Preparing for graduation was exciting! I was happy, nervous- just a ball of emotions. Walking the hall as a SENIOR just felt different, especially as a teenage mom! I wasn't the only teenage mom in high school, but everyone's story was different. I can only share my own personal thoughts and struggles. Being able to engage in all of the senior activities and take beautiful senior pictures was an amazing milestone to cross. I didn't order a class ring or anything extra, just my cap and gown. I was happy with just that. I was grateful that my family didn't force me to miss those things because of my baby.

I had plenty of family support for my graduation. My grandma [Ruth], dad [Tony] and stepmom [Rose] along with their four children [Toni, Amanda, Dominique, and Clotelia] came from Chicago to join in with my mom's side of the family and my friends in Blytheville. It was totally amazing to have everyone together supporting me during this significant milestone of my life! Their excited cheers for me walking across the football field to accept my diploma was an awe-inspiring moment for all of us! Life could've taken a horrible turn for me, but it didn't. I persistently continued on a piece of the path God had for me, regardless of the personal hiccups I incurred. For many, I was probably written off as another typical "hood" statistic, but I had no doubt in my mind that I would successfully graduate. I felt blessed to have made it that far, especially with the background I had. Strength must've been my middle name because whenever the time came, I managed to rise to the occasion. I remember a time when people were saying I was going to have kids back-to-back and drop out of school, but I was determined to put that theory in the grave. Even if I didn't want to be strong or better myself, I had to do it anyway. Life wasn't just about me anymore. I loved being a mom. My son was making me a better person each day.

With my mom rebounding from the streets and returning into our lives, we were not having to continue living with my grandparents much longer. My mom got on her feet and secured a place for her and all of us [her children]. We moved into a nice three-bedroom, light- brown brick house that sat behind the parking lot of a school [not quite sure if it was elementary or kindergarten]. By this time, she had been home from prison for a while with a heart set on moving forward on a positive path.

Just reflecting and writing about it, I remember it being the greatest feeling in the world to be at home with our mom on a full-time basis. She wasted no time picking up where she'd left off a few years ago. She was very present and always took very good care of us! She worked long and arduous hours at a factory. In return for her going out of the way providing for us, I took over the domestic role with my siblings by cooking meals, cleaning the house, and readying them for school.

She trusted me and actually felt safe with the new guy I was talking to at that time. However, I'm not sure if she ever totally agreed or liked it, but he stayed over our house plenty of nights while she was working. I guess she just felt safe with him being there because she worked nights and we lived in a corner house tucked away behind the school with little outside lighting. He was about 10 years my senior, tall, dark, and handsome. He had wavy hair which he maintained in a low haircut. He was a pretty good guy overall and took care of us. The biggest issue I had with him was that he snorted powder [i.e., cocaine]. When he and I first met and made it past the small talk and into the bed, one of us gave the other an STD [sexually transmitted disease]. With both of us having been promiscuous, neither of us knew which was the carrier; however, we got it medically taken care of and continued having a relationship.

Things were great between us until his habits got worse. The more he continued snorting and popping pills, the more paranoid he became. His paranoia eventually led to a couple of disturbing actions perpetrated by him. The first occurred when he and my "bestie" conspired a lie in an attempt to set me up. She lied to him, stating some very hurtful things I was supposed to have said. Honestly, I don't even remember what it was that I supposedly said. But I do recall being super hurt because of that ordeal. It was a deep-hearted, personal hurt because I believe it was purposely done with an intent to damage my character. What made matters worse was when I found out they BOTH were in on it. I was never able to trust either of them ever again. These were the two people I was around EVERY SINGLE DAY! To this day, I don't understand what their reasoning was behind such a reprehensible act. I can only assume that it may have been induced by drugs on both their parts. I did eventually forgive them, but the trust issue remained.

Another example of his paranoia occurred at times when he would anxiously walk around the house with a gun and sleep with it under the pillow as if someone was looking for him. He would sit in the dark and listen to the rap group *Three 6 mafia* repeatedly on my mom's huge speakers that were sitting in the living room, all the while popping pills. I assumed they were ecstasy pills. He never tried to hurt us, but his behavior mixed with my "best" friend's lies and personal issues were overwhelming, and I couldn't do it anymore. I've had my share of demons in my life but was never drawn to drama created by others. I ended that relationship but continued to have my share of "friends" here and there - nothing serious until baby number 2 was conceived.

Reflecting on it all, I see clearly why I didn't like dealing with the drama others brought into my life, but I couldn't see the drama I was living and creating for my own life. I was blinded by pain, low self-esteem, a misguided life, no proper mentor, lack of a relationship with and knowledge about God, and an environment that thrived on all the wrong things that choked out the real purpose for living. The candidness of what I share is by no means a boast about foolishness. It's to take you through the unconscious affairs of someone [me] searching for purpose and what really matters in life to the best of my abilities. Sadly, the experiences aren't pretty at all, but there was something inside of me [possibly placed there by the prayers of my grandparents and/or others] that would not allow me to give up and kept me on the search for whatever greater purpose there was out there for me to encounter. Yet, there were more dreadful experiences forthcoming before I would attain that purpose. But God!

Chapter 17

My Baby, What Happened?

◇◇◇◇◇◇◇◇◇◇◇◇

U p until 2008, I was the mother of only one amazing son! That is the year another bundle of joy had been made [i.e., I got pregnant]. I'd met my second child's father, through a mutual friend, when I was roughly about 18 years old. During our initial meeting, we gelled with one another very well – but in a brother and sister like manner. Because of that, it was rather strange of us being physically attracted to one another. He was a total package and humorously kept me entertained. Publicly, we never made known or interacted as though we were in a relationship; however, behind closed doors it was more than evident.

The secret relations we were having behind closed doors became the cause of my second pregnancy. In this case, it wasn't an over-the-counter pregnancy test or medical appointment that confirmed the pregnancy. I was able to discern based on the soreness and growth of my breasts – definitely, far beyond the normal small boobs I previously had. Eventually, I took a pregnancy test and sure enough the result was positive! I was excited! I really can't explain why because we were not in a relationship, it wasn't a planned pregnancy, and I had not considered the struggles of being a single mother of two. When I first told him [boyfriend], he was ECSTATIC as well! He bragged about how beautiful his "baby's Mom" [being me] was and couldn't keep his hands off my belly, even though I wasn't showing at that time. Things were going great!

During the time of that pregnancy, I worked at Wal-Mart. One day while at work as a sales associate in the Electronics department, I started to bleed. Luckily, there were no customers in line as I took a break to go to the bathroom to examine and clean myself. I didn't freak out nor become too alarmed because I've heard of this happening before during pregnancies by others. Also, I recently had a medical appointment and was told by the physician that everything was fine during the routine pregnancy exam. Immediately after work, I did call and schedule an appointment for another physical exam.

The next day upon attending and completing the medical examination, it was officially determined by the physician that I had suffered a miscarriage. I was devastated, to say the least! That was a most difficult time for me, which made me very sad and depressed, partly because I couldn't understand why it happened. I'd never known death until I received the news of having a miscarriage. One moment you, as a mother, have a living being growing within you. You're happy, planning, and full of life as you oftentimes find yourself imagining life with this child. The next moment, it's like you've been punched directly in the heart by a heavyweight boxer. You're left breathless, hurt, and alone. Many times, you try to put the pieces of how, what, when, and why together to make sense of it all, and there's no comforting answer. That's what I refer to as an uncertainty of life – anything can happen at anytime, and as much as we want to blame someone, that blame will never recompense the pain and grief nor make things right. There's when the seed of faith I had placed in God's hand helped get me through.

I called my boyfriend from the hospital to share the news, but his phone kept going straight to voicemail. While at the hospital and when I arrived home, I'd repeatedly called and left him several voicemail messages – this went on for several days, but he never returned any of my calls. I finally got the 'hint' that it was his way of breaking up with me. Imagine going through a miscarriage and a "breakup" at the same time! I had no idea what caused his change of heart. Anyway, the next few weeks, I lived life wearing shaded glasses because I didn't want anyone to see the pain in my eyes. The suffering pain was because of the miscarriage, feeling alone/abandoned, and negative thoughts about myself physically as well as about how my life was going.

Six months later, guess who decided to contact me?! Yes, out of the blue, he decided to randomly text me - SIX MONTHS LATER. The message he texted was a pitiful excuse of why he'd been avoiding contact with me. It read, "I wasn't sure if the baby was mine." My natural response was, "What?!" As if that was a legitimate reason to abandon us! I know I had a rough and questionable past, but this time was different. I was 100% SURE that he was the father! And, if his only concern was knowing for sure he was the father, abandonment wasn't the way to resolve it. We could've easily gotten a paternity test completed. He was the ONLY guy I was intimate with during the entire time of our "secret" relationship. The whole situation triggered distressing feelings and thoughts from my past. Feelings of being used and unwanted! I questioned how this could be happening to me again. I had changed – at least I believed I was on a better path toward change! Time went on, our relationship deteriorated, and I was back to my old ways.

The disappointment I kept finding in guys and love was the result of me not realizing I was in a dis-appointed [out of place] relationship with God. I was so bent on recklessly spreading and planting my affections and emotions among those I thought were good potentials for making me whole; yet they were worse off than I was and totally incapable of filling the void in my life – this I now know. It would take a long while and many more unwise experiences for me to get where I am now. But, God!

Chapter 18

An Escapable Trap

◇◇◇◇◇◇◇◇◇

After the situations regarding the miscarriage and the "secret" relationship breakup, my life seemed to have spiraled out of control and down the wrong road. Why so? I guess it was familiar territory. My years as a teen had paved the course of negative culture that I had become all too comfortable with. No one was to blame but myself. Being an adult, I couldn't displace the blame on my mother, grandparents, or anyone else. It sucks being a female adult, having to walk blindly and feel your way through life – especially when you become numb to emotional hurt by men and lack of knowledge about life and God. Although I was hurt by my miscarriage and unfortunate men issues, I was completely aware of my actions moving forward. Just as the decisions before, so were the decisions after – they were choices I made!

Soon after the miscarriage and breakup incidents, I went hard down the path of promiscuity. I felt like if God cared, He could've prevented a lot of what I was going through. So by me doing what I was doing, right or wrong, He either didn't care or allowed it to be for whatever reason.

Prior to getting pregnant with my third child, I was sexually intimate with several guys, including the guy who broke my virginity, his brother, and one of his cousins. Yes, you read that correctly! I NEVER intended to go that route, but I think the feeling of being wanted by ANYONE just excited me (in actuality, the driving force was the feeling of being unwanted and unloved). Having someone treat me as if they really liked me (whether pretentiously or not), was uplifting.

The guy who broke my virginity [in the back of his mother's van] had made plans for us to move away together and just start this amazing new life! He really laid the plan out believably thick. I was excited and ready for a real relationship with him, so I agreed! Shortly after and in the midst of making plans for our lives going forward, I found out he was cheating by sleeping around with other women. His cousin and cousin's girlfriend had already told me, but it was confirmed when I popped up at the house of another family member of his and saw a woman sitting on his lap. I shouldn't have been surprised, but I was deeply hurt. Out of that hurt and anger, a door was opened for an unimaginable act.

Because of the troubles he and I had, which resulted in another break-up, his brother and I began spending time together. His brother was cute, and I liked him as a person, but our relationship was strictly platonic. Eventually during an innocent hangout, his brother and I gave into subtle temptations, leading to us having unprotected sex a couple of times. Inexcusably, I was acting out of hurt. Personally, I believe my actions hurt me more than anyone else. Unfortunately, that hurt didn't deter me from doing more disgraceful acts.

Their cousin was the next guy I slept with. We all used to hang together over at his cousin's girlfriend's house. I LOVED her and their kids. We used to all cook, drink and just hang out as chummy friends. Their kids always would refer to me as "auntie". I used to spend the night with her [cousin's girlfriend] while he [cousin] was away. Our friendship was EVERYTHING you'd imagine a friendship should be! Indeed, it was; that was, until along came a dastardly opportunity.

One evening after visiting with him [the cousin], his girlfriend, and a few others at his [the cousin's] apartment, I was getting tired, and it was getting late, so I decided to depart. As I was leaving, he [the cousin] offered to give me a ride home. I only stayed around the corner, but I accepted his offer anyway. On the way home, he told me that he had a crush on me. Although flattered, I didn't know exactly what to think or say because I'd always considered him and his girlfriend as very good and close friends. Meeting and knowing him earlier on, he was the only respectable one out of the bunch of guys I'd known (that used to hang outside the apartment complex) who never tried to holler at me, grab my backside, etc etc. I liked that about him but nothing beyond. To top it off, he was the boyfriend of one of my best friend girls. I have never intentionally hurt people or broke up relationships or homes.

Even though I knew it was wrong, we did exchange phone numbers and began a "secret" relationship on the side – all while I was still hanging with his girlfriend [a "best" friend of mine]. It was a terrible situation by so many accounts, but foremost because I really did love her and their children. So why did I continue in the "secret" relationship with her boyfriend? He was really good to me and didn't treat me like everyone else had in the past. Even before we became intimate, when I had found out I was pregnant and shared this info with him, he didn't care. Yes, that should have told me something was wrong with both of us right then! However, as time went on, our feelings grew stronger as we indulged in sexual activities with one another. His girlfriend eventually found out and the friendship between she and I was ruined. He and I continued our relationship no matter how anyone around us felt about it. He even started believing that my unborn child was his. He was very supportive by going to every prenatal medical appointment with me. At one point, he'd suggested I say the baby is his to eliminate all of the extra drama and people involved. As good as that sounded, I couldn't do it. My life was filled with enough lies.

Granted, many of you may say this whole situation is totally unusual and not something anyone can see God in. And you're right! However, I've come to learn that God doesn't have to be in the midst of something bad for Him to use it for good later. There are many times and occasions throughout our lives when He places a call on our lives that we answer "yes" to. He then takes all of the past mistakes, heartbreaks, and headaches and makes use of them as teaching, learning, and testimonial tools.

In 2009, baby number three, Key'Essence, was born. My rainbow baby! Her real father and I went to high school together. I had a mad crush on and was very physically attracted to him. He was slightly taller than me and slim built with a CHOCOLATE complexion. We connected through mutual friends, which immediately led to a one-night stand. We were both cool with it. After our one night of pleasure, we went back to our regular separate lives. He was doing his thing, as was I. Key'Essence was born December of 2009 via C-section. My Mom was with me at the hospital during her birth. This birth was much easier than the first one. Unlike the first pregnancy, I now knew what to expect. I was scheduled to be induced December 25th but she came early, at about 34 ½ weeks. She entered the world weighing five pounds and 15 ounces. Just as she was a baby, she is today – a beautiful chocolate drop. She was born with a light complexion, pink lips, big beautiful brown eyes, and curly brown hair.

Being a single parent, life with two children wasn't too bad. I quickly made necessary adjustments for the benefit of all three of us as a whole. They were great children, so that made things much easier. We also still lived with my mother, which was a huge help. At the time, not knowing who her real Dad was had begun eating me up inside. I decided to contact each of the potential fathers to inform them of the possibility of one of them being the father. Luckily, they all took it well and there was no negative or mean-spirited confrontation. We were adults and aware of the consequences of our negligent sexual actions. They all agreed to move forward with a blood test. However, there was only one who took the test – the one who I suspected the most and who my friends said she looked most like. When the test came back, it was no surprise to me; he [the guy I knew from high school] was the father! That's right, the one I had slept with ONE TIME! This situation felt kind of familiar. Even after confirmation, he wasn't super present in her life. Not to make excuses for him, but I'm quite sure he needed time to process it as much as I did. Remember we linked up one time and didn't really have an ongoing line of communication. Life wasn't easy but I was taking accountability for my actions and attempting to do right by everyone this time around.

I moved into my first place after my second child. It was a brick house with three bedrooms and one bathroom. It was located on a corner facing an empty field. It wasn't a fancy place, but it was clean, spacious, and most importantly, MINE! I loved everything about that house besides the fact that it had window units, instead of central heat and air, and MICE. Lots of mice! We used to exterminate 3-4 mice daily. They were small but I didn't care. They served no purpose in my home and I wanted them gone! I wasn't sure if it was infested before I moved in or if they were coming from the field across the street (or possibly both). After some time, I had gotten used to them. There were too many and they won. I was still fearful but did my best to keep the place clean and plug any noticeable entry points they may have been using to get in. I did that until we could move to another affordable place. Besides the mice, everything in that house was going good until noises of scratching behind the walls and cabinets seemed to get louder. I wasn't too sure whether it was a group of mice scratching at one time or one huge rat.

One day, I was home alone. I'd been hearing the scratching for a while, but this time it seemed to have gained traction and had become closer than usual. I slowly walked from the back of the house to the kitchen. As I slowly peeked around the doorway entrance, what did I see??? A freakin' opossum sitting on top of my fridge! I was terrified! I grabbed my cell phone and called Mom with the quickness! She hurriedly walked from her house to mine. It was a cloudy day and looked as though it could rain any minute. Luckily it did not start raining before she got there (it was a lengthy walk, and I had her vehicle). I was too scared to get the keys to her vehicle off the table in the kitchen! The opossum kept falling behind and climbing up the back of the refrigerator. I believed it was either a baby, or maybe a teenage opossum – if you know what I mean. It was medium-sized and very scary looking.

When Mom arrived, we called 911. Too funny, right? She came all the way over to my house and was just as scared as I was! That's my mom; when she's down with you, she'll dependably stand beside you. After the 911 call, we stayed on our phones calling friends and family in disbelief of what was going on. By it occurring on a Saturday, the Humane Society was closed; otherwise, that would have been our first call. The police arrived and got the opossum out with a box very quickly. They laughed at us, which I thought was sort of rude, but brushed it off. In my mind, all I could think was that if a baby opossum was in the house, the mom and/or dad had to be close. Luckily, I never saw any more in the house at all.

Chapter 19

Bad Habits, But Getting Better

◇◇◇◇◇◇◇◇◇◇◇◇◇◇

B eing a single Mom of two children with two different Daddies wasn't too difficult of a job to maintain, albeit not the ideal situation for any woman to be in; however, what was done couldn't be undone. The only difficulty was not having a real relationship with either of their fathers. But things could've been worse. And indeed, things did get worse. By this time, you've probably guessed what it was – another pregnancy! That's exactly what 2010 had in store for me - pregnant AGAIN! Here's one for you that you may not have guessed. Who's the father this time? None other than…the guy I was pregnant by which ended in a miscarriage. How did we even link up again after that ordeal?

Over the course of time, out of the blue, he contacted me. We began with catch up small talk for breaking the ice and calming the emotions from our past relationship. This time around he had a girlfriend, but he portrayed that home life was going really bad. That was the open door for us restarting to vibe.

It was also the open door for us reengaging in sexual activity with one another. One particular time he came into my home and jokingly said, "Four baby mama's? Ok, that's not bad." That led me to believe he was purposely going to try to impregnate me. Immediately after that statement, we went at it. I had foolishly given in without further consideration of becoming pregnant. As soon as we finished, he told me I was pregnant. Strangely, he didn't seem too bothered about it, which resulted in me feeling a little better about this possible pregnancy. Days later and after several home tests, the results CONFIRMED that I was, in fact, pregnant. My answer to that confirmation was…"Noooo!" Three baby Daddies?! By the age of 23?…Ummm, no! It totally sent me into a deep depression and the initiation of an appointment at the local abortion clinic. So, I go from being distraught over a miscarriage to willfully ready to abort. By this time, I am confused on so many levels.

There I was, pregnant for the fourth time! I wasn't in a relationship and already had two absent fathers. What was I thinking and why wasn't I thinking? This is the same man who ghosted me with my first pregnancy, when I needed him! That point in my life was overwhelmingly depressing. I found myself laying on the couch for days on end. I'd lost all interest in life. I didn't want to eat, wasn't in my normal chipper mood, and definitely didn't want any company. I'd be the first to tell anyone that depression is a real mental health issue than can and will truly drive you to doing things you never thought you could or would ever do. I knew that I had to pull myself together, but how? I just wanted to somehow get rid of the baby and move on as though that incident never happened.

Growing up in church did shape my non-belief in abortions. However, all of that was getting ready to go out of the window. I did not want another child! I selfishly thought about my previous pregnancies and encounters with guys. I selfishly thought about what people would say about me. There I was, an adult and in my own place, and yet I was incapable of making mature decisions. The decisions I was making were all selfish and ending with dire consequences. As in times before, I would mingle prayer and worry in search for an answer to alleviate the pain in my life. Neither worked for this double-minded woman. What I needed was for my life to be completely overhauled and only God could do that – but I still didn't catch the hint!

I had finally made my decision about baby number three. I wanted and decided on an abortion. I asked the dad for money toward the abortion, and he declined. He said he didn't believe in abortions. How asinine is that? He didn't believe in abortions, but he was okay neglecting Daddy responsibilities in raising a child. Anyhow, I decided to take matters into my own hands. I called the abortion clinic to schedule an appointment and went online to get a loan. I got approved for the loan and made a point of not touching the funds once they hit my bank account. I've never been a smart money manager, but I was adamant about not touching that money. Sometimes we think we have life all figured out, then GOD shows up like "Not so fast! We're going to do it MY WAY."

As the abortion appointment was fast approaching, I went to the bank to double check that the funds were still intact and accessible. To my shocking disbelief, they were gone! I had not touched the money at all, so I didn't know what was going on. Now, I'm really freaking out because I knew that I would have to cancel my appointment. There was no way I was going to be able to get ahold of that amount of money in time; and the clinic wouldn't do the abortion after a certain number of weeks. That whole situation had me devastated. I told my baby's dad and he seemed glad things didn't work out that way.

As time went on, I started to feel a little better about my situation because, surprisingly, the dad was present. He would come over almost every day and rub my belly. I remember one time he teared up while we were riding and talking about the child. Well, that euphoric episode didn't last too long. Ironically, he and his girlfriend started to do better, so he stopped coming around. He was no longer present to witness the growth of my belly or any of the special pregnancy moments. He would call every now and then and I would send him pictures, but it wasn't the same. He wasn't there during her birth but did reappear after her birth. When the time came for me to give birth, I was alone. My Mom and sister [Cora] were with me during the early part of the day but had to leave and be somewhere else later that afternoon. Moments after their departure, it was time to deliver. She was born approximately an hour after they departed.

I went into labor with my newborn, Bre'Elle, on the day I was scheduled to have her. I drove myself up the street to the hospital that morning, which was about five minutes away, like most places in small-town Blytheville. This pregnancy was much easier than the previous two because I was now sort of an "expert" on what to expect and had awareness of what complications could arise – I was sort of in a comfortable, "I got this" zone. In fact, I was so comfortable in this situation that I was able to be on my phone in between contractions! The room was cold like all hospitals typically are; but unlike before, I didn't jump during the epidural injection; I was able to control my breathing, and I was wide awake! I actually felt and experienced the complete birth of Bre'Elle, not pain, just lots of pressure. She was born via C-section just as my other two children were. My "titty" baby came into the world weighing six pounds and 10 ounces. I call her my "titty" baby because she was and still is very much attached to me. I don't know if it was because I breastfed her or because God knew I needed that special relationship and connection with her on the road to Him filling the void in my life. She had tight eyes and smooth, dark brown hair. Her hair was mostly straight with a few curls.

My stay in the hospital was only a few days. During the stay, her dad and his aunt visited her and me. He and I were in a better place as friends but were no longer contemplating being together or having any relations. He would come by and even spend the night sometimes at my house. I remember him saying "I know she's mine," as if he was trying to convince himself that she was. This lasted for a few months, then the next thing I knew he was requesting a paternity test. As a matter of fact, she looks so much like him [and always has], that I've had people ask me if she was my daughter, because she looks nothing like me. I was upset about him requesting a paternity test, but I had to and did respect his decision. He said he just wanted to make sure she was his. Unlike with my first two children, I wasn't stressed about these results because I knew what the outcome would be 99.99%. Sure enough, the paternity test result confirmed just that!

Although my relationship status seemed to be "eternally single," I was happy. I loved being a mom so much! It made me feel alive by giving me purpose for someone who was mine [my children]. We had a better house, a good routine. I worked great hours at the Head-start center my daughters were attending, so everything was good. There was only one thing that really kept lingering in my head – the fact that I decided to get my tubes tied, cut, and burned. I went back and forth about it several times before making a final decision to do so. One part of me said and questioned, "No. You might get married one day and what if y'all want kids?" The other part of me said, "Girl, now you know how you are, get those tubes tied!" Aside from not wanting to chance having a fourth random Baby Daddy, I was concerned about the health risks because I had already had three C-sections. The thought of having a fourth C-section really scared me. I made the decision to get my tubes tied, cut, and burned. Afterward, sure enough I did meet the man who would eventually become my husband when Bre'Elle was 11 months old. Regrets about the tied tubes took over my body.

We as humans make numerous mistakes and foolish decisions to the point where we discount what God is capable of overcoming. We allow condemnation to define us, people to judge us, and failure to become us. As long as we have breath in our bodies, a heart that beats, and a mind to think, God still calls, forgives, blesses, and is there to put us on track. Our mess is just that, mess! We're not meant to wallow in it, make light of it, or make a lifestyle of it – we're built for coming out of it. For some of us it takes a little longer, and a lot of learning from more bad experiences…But, God!

Chapter 20

And, Then My Love Came Along

<><><><><><><><><><><><><><><>

T here seems to come a time in one's life when you stop searching for what you've been looking for and just go with the flow. It's in those times that fate takes its course and catches you off guard by placing what you've previously been on the hunt for (but have given up on) directly before your eyes. So it was in my case. One evening in January 2012, there was a group of us out celebrating my mom's birthday at a lounge in Blytheville called Bistro 1121. I was wearing a short, black dress with heels and standing near my mom sharing laughs. While we were preparing to get our night started, a local biker group called, "Full Throttle" came into the lounge. One of the guys quickly made his way over to me and simply asked me for a hug. He was average height and dark-complexioned with dreads. He was wearing jeans, a white t-shirt, and his black biker vest. We had never met before, but I obliged him with a hug. He must've needed and enjoyed it because he asked for another one directly after. Afterward, he went back to the group of bikers he'd come with.

Upon initially meeting him, I thought to myself that he was "okay." He was far from the usual type of guys I'd meet and hook up with. I was used to "bad boys," and he seemed pretty strait laced – not nerdy nor thuggish. About a month went by before we ever talked again. One day my coworker [Kendra], who was in the biker group with him, stopped me as if she was glad to see me. She stopped me and said, "Giiirrll, I'm so glad I found you! Jaybird (whose real name was Brandon) has been asking for your number since the night he saw you. Can I give it to him?" I instantly knew who she was talking about, although we never officially introduced ourselves that night at Bistro. At the time, I was talking to the married guy who I had a pregnancy scare with at age 18 (yes, we reconnected). However, I decided to give her my number to give to him [Jaybird]. Side note is that he remembers it oppositely. He says I got his number from her first. Either way, we somehow got one another's number. It didn't take long for us to start talking. After our first conversation, we talked on the phone every day and night for hours on end. We talked about everything. I was excited to know more about him and to tell him more about me. It was so refreshing to have the feeling I was experiencing through conversations with him. This was the first time I'd ever felt like somebody wanted to get to know me for me without expecting anything in return.

According to him, upon seeing me for the first time, his first thought was "Dang, she fine!" He always describes the sparks he felt when we first hugged. I take it as love at first sight, or maybe a strong 'like' mixed with lust. I felt bad because initially I didn't feel anything, but once we started conversing on the phone, feelings of attraction arose quickly. It didn't take long for me to tell him about my past and he never judged me! That is one thing I love and appreciate about him to this day. He has never made me feel like I was less than or only good for one thing.

After a couple weeks of hanging out, we decided to link up to watch a movie at my apartment. He remembers me cooking potatoes and barbecue pork steaks that night – he considered it my specialty. He has great memory. He remembers so many things about our courtship that I embarrassingly can't remember. About the only memory I have of him at my house during those times was the night we were intimate – which was the second time we hung out. I vividly remember us watching a movie and waiting for another friend of mine to come over. For whatever reason, this night we both were feeling a little hot and bothered. Prior to her coming over, we had our very first kiss, with tongue! I was so happy when she pulled up because I didn't want things to go any further. It was too early in our relationship, and I didn't want to ruin things. I was so used to just being a 'sex buddy.' God knows that I didn't want the same with him.

Well, Kendra arrived, and we were all small talking and finishing up watching whatever movie we were engaged in. However, after having that spectacular mind-blowing kiss, our minds were somewhere else other than the movie. So, guess what? Kendra being there didn't stop anything. We were sitting on different couches – Kendra on one couch and Jaybird and I on another. Hormones got the best of us both, and suddenly he led me into the bedroom, where we started doing the do – not caring about Kendra being in the living room. He and I jokingly say it was that "sample" that led us to marriage. He told me later that he believed I would have been pregnant that night if not for my tubes being tied, cut, and burned.

Although we had a good time that night, a weighty feeling of guilt had come upon me as well as doubt about his interest in me. I just KNEW he wasn't going to call again, probably label me as 'easy' and not talk to me anymore after that night. Man, was I wrong! We continued dating.

One incident I remember and still cherish, is when we spent the night over his brother's house in Osceola, Arkansas. It was the female "time of the month" for me, and I figured he wouldn't want to spend the weekend with me because of that. My head immediately filled with those negative thoughts derived from past relationships with guys who only wanted me for sex. Turned out that it was all in my head as we had the best weekend! We partied and just got to know more about one another. There was one thing that happened which threw me off. There was a girl he was talking to at the party who was an ex-girlfriend. My intuition told me that before he did, but I didn't say anything. I assume he either felt guilty or noticed my demeanor change because when we got into the car, he held my hand and repeatedly told me how sorry he was; I forgave him.

We were inseparable. We hadn't made things official yet, but our actions said otherwise. We both were talking to other people, but I don't see how we had time for anyone else between working, partying every weekend, and hanging out together nearly every day. It wasn't long before we made things official – to be exact, the date was February 28, 2012. We were setting up for my daughter's [Bre'Elle] first birthday party and he got a phone call. I'm not sure who It was but I remember him saying, "I'm at my girl house setting up for the baby's party." They must have asked where he was. I was in awe! I was excited, because not only were my feelings super strong, but this was my first REAL boyfriend. I couldn't wait to dip off and tell my bestie. That same day, I texted all my boy toys and CUT THEM OFF! They were not happy about it. Some even begged me not to. I didn't care or have any second thoughts behind it. I finally had a BOYFRIEND! Wow!

Things were hot and heavy for the first year of our relationship, even in the midst of cheating. There were times I found sexual text messages in his phone between he and other females and even caught him on the phone talking to some of them. Ask him and he would say he never cheated on me, but everyone has their own perceptions of what constitutes cheating. I was so upset; especially since we talked about having an open relationship – to include threesomes – and he declined, saying he only wanted to be with me. My question then was, "Why try to cheat?"

I was far from innocent myself. I had cheated with two other guys during the first part of our relationship, but deeply regretted doing so. Adding fuel to the fire, I had also cheated around with my next-door neighbor. I didn't think he would care because it was with a girl. Identifying as bisexual was something he liked about me when we first met. Although he and I never had any joint encounters with females, I had plenty and really enjoyed that lifestyle at that time. What I didn't know until later was just how wrong I was about him not caring. I'd come to learn directly from him how hurt he was about the chosen bisexual lifestyle and how he questioned himself on whether he satisfied me enough. I was truly happy with him. I quickly got my mind right and started to be 100% faithful. I assumed he did the same.

Wanting someone, or just simply to be accepted, will cause you to accept and do things without thinking. When that occurs, we can best believe and know who's working such confusion – the enemy of God and mankind! Looking through the rear-view mirror, it's easy to identify what was going on, but when you're in the midst of the mess, things seem so normal.

Chapter 21

Makeup to Breakup

◇◇◇◇◇◇◇◇◇

A little under a year of dating and living together, he finally proposed. I knew it was coming soon because he talked about it often - I just didn't know when. He said things like, "I'm going to make you my wife," or "It's coming sooner than you think." All I knew is that I was committed and READY! In February 2013, we went out for dinner on Valentine's Day. In my heart, I KNEW that was going to be the day. Dinner was awesome! Our whole night was smooth and on point. To my surprise, that night did NOT end in a proposal. I was a little disappointed yet still happy to be in a committed relationship.

It wasn't until the very next day that he popped the question. He was coming from work, and I was at a local sports store in Blytheville. He texted and asked where I was. After I told him, he drove over and parked in the store's parking lot. I went and sat in the car with him and was just running my mouth about much of nothing. Suddenly, I was speechless upon noticing the ring sitting on the armrest! My exact words were, "Stop playing!" He definitely was not playing. I couldn't believe nor could've ever imagined that I was about to be somebody's wife! This is something I felt strongly about - especially since I believed a stronger/closer relationship with God was coming into fruition. I've always had a strong desire to do things the right way, but the flesh would always trip me up. It was then that I realized that God could get our attention by touching our hearts through the foolishness of our shortcomings.

We immediately started the wedding plans. Neither of us were really picky so it wasn't difficult at all. I'm sure he got tired of me asking about colors and flowers, though. It was starting to be a bit much financially and emotionally, so we decided to do a courthouse wedding and plan the real thing at a later and more affordable time.

On April 5, 2013, we tied the knot! We had a courthouse ceremony with my sister, Cora, as the witness. Our "honeymoon" consisted of us going to eat at Olive Garden in Jonesboro, Arkansas and getting a hotel afterwards. It may not sound like much to most, but it meant everything to me – someone who was been longing to be accepted and loved. We were happy and our night was perfect! Married life was great, until it wasn't. I think we both came into it with certain expectations and individual views. Our relationship became like a rollercoaster, up and down. Marriage was what I wanted but not prepared for. It was something else in life that I wasn't taught nor smart about. In 2014, my kids and I moved to Jonesboro. Jaybird and I talked about moving there but he changed his mind at the last minute. I can only guess that the reason he didn't come with us was the uncertainty of our relationship.

Chapter 22

Where Do We Go From Here?

◇◇◇◇◇◇◇◇◇◇◇◇◇◇◇

L ife without Jaybird was bittersweet. On one hand I was doing "my thang", working two jobs and in a decent little apartment. On the other hand, I wanted my husband there with me. During that separation, the devil wearing the disguise of our flesh entered with old habits that were lain to the side but not put to death. We both formed relationships with other people. I returned to a bisexual lifestyle, talking to a girl I worked with, and he was talking to a girl who graduated high school with me. Eventually, he and I reconnected as friends. It was crazy because our friendship outside of marriage was THE BEST! We talked about EVERYTHING, even about our new partners. In 2015, realizing we really missed one another and wanting to make things work, he finally moved and joined the kids and I in Jonesboro. Once again things were hot and heavy, and I'm not just talking sexual relations. We have always had this electrifying connection. Whenever we are around one another, sparks fly!

From 2016 to 2018, we were back in forth in our relationship. I think we moved separately every year, up until 2018 when we filed for divorce. We had gotten to a point where communication was no longer happening. It was very unfortunate, too, because communication had always been our strong suit. However, we had grown apart by not talking for days and weeks at a time as well as never addressing our unresolved problems. Every small problem felt HUGE because we never worked them out and allowed them to be blown out of proportion. For instance, there was one night when we had major miscommunication, leading to him staying out ALL NIGHT until about 9am the next morning, with no calls or texts. I was LIVID! When he finally came home, I calmly told him to get out. I didn't want to talk to him AT ALL! My mind was all over the place. I didn't know whether he was out cheating or if he truly did get drunk and fall asleep on someone's couch like he stated. That, mixed with our other unresolved problems put the icing on the cake for me. We were separated for 6 months before we officially divorced. By this time, I was calm and didn't want to, but he was done with me.

Sometimes the things we pray for and get, are things we aren't mature enough to handle. They then become experiences of trouble, hurt, and pain that show us we weren't ready. A spiritually immature person searching for God will only see what they perceive is from God. God's will is wrapped in our surrendering to Him, something I did not know nor was prepared to do at that time.

We filed for divorce September 2018, with it being finalized in October 2018. The night before we filed, I stayed the night at his place. Quite odd, right? He grilled us some steaks, we watched movies and cuddled. That next morning, we went our separate ways and decided to meet up at the courthouse later that day. We met at the courthouse, held hands upon entering and exiting. I repeatedly told him that it wasn't too late for us to change our minds. He was uncertain as well, because the love and natural spark was still there, but we went forth with it anyway. We talked on the phone that same day and just went back to our regular, individual routines. The longest period we hadn't talked to one another was about a month. Somehow and some way, we seemingly always found our way back to one another. We tried to talk and work things out several times and failed, but that didn't stop us from staying connected. I can't put my finger on what it is that keeps us connected, but it is what it is.

During our divorce, we both were in the process of moving on. I had started talking to this guy I met in Memphis through an online website. Jaybird started talking to a girl in California and was contemplating on moving there. Not sure how they met or how long they knew one another. Illogically, our separate lives seemed pretty good, but we still hooked up for dates and sex from time to time. This went on for two years! In 2020, we decided to reconcile for good. We talked about EVERYTHING! Especially the old stuff and what led to our divorce. About a month after laying everything out on the table, we decided to move back in together [July 2020]. It wasn't a hard transition because the love connection we shared was never lost. My family loves him and, most importantly, he and I naturally love one another. As excited as I was, my spirit was convicting me. I figured he would marry me soon, so I didn't have too much longer to feel guilty about shacking up. After all, we tremendously missed one another, missed being in the house together, missed the dates, family times etc. Whenever problems arose, this time around, we valued and utilized communication. After about a year, we still weren't married, and my spirit was still convicting me. Wanting to do what is right by God, I brought it to his attention that I wanted to live in separate homes until further notice. He said he understood 100% and we both complied. Although the conversation of marriage had subsided, we still had that undeniable spark for one another. In my heart, I believed and trusted that God was definitely at work with our union.

Chapter 23

God Is There

<><><><><><>

With more than 33 years of my life having been a portrait made up of splattered paint, little did I know it was actually to become a beautiful mess. Throughout those many years, my life had not been perfect, by far. Although my life was comprised of splattered paint, God would soon become the maestro and bring value to my life portrait. There isn't a specific moment that I can remember having an encounter with GOD, because I've always believed He has been with me. When I was sleeping around, "shacking up", partying etc., He knew where I was and what I was up to. He has placed in each of us a measure of faith and I, like many others, oftentimes placed the faith in failed relationships rather than focusing it on Him. Morally, I believe He has also placed within each of us knowledge of right and wrong. Those right and wrong convictions represent His presence. Most times, I ignored those convictions and other times I heeded them.

He has been and continues blessing me with mercy and grace. Giving me opportunity after opportunity to repent and surrender totally to Him. I'm at a place of understanding that I can no longer base my salvation and relationship with God on simply going to or growing up in the church. Repentance is making a commitment to trust and receive Jesus as my Lord and Savior, turning away from the ungodly things I was accustomed to doing, and grabbing a hold of His love and will for my life. As I got older, I learned to separate the "religion" aspect and work towards building an actual relationship with Him. I remember being so stressed out and thinking that the moment I do something wrong, God is just going to strike me dead and send me straight to hell. I still have some of those moments of conviction, but I also know that He has a plan for my life, a perfect plan. That doesn't mean that my journey or every decision I make will be perfect, and that's ok. He is not waking me up every day just to waste time or just for me to pay bills and die. My purpose is greater than my natural eye can see.

For a long time, I looked at God as a "punisher" of some sort. I was so scared to mess up in life that it elevated my anxiety to another level. However, I gain peace by having daily conversations with Him, which gives me the reassurance that I need. I am reminded of His love, grace and will. No matter what people say or think of me nor how crazy the world gets, I know that He is still waking me up because He is not done with me yet. Do I still have issues I am dealing with? Certainly! But I am grateful that He is patiently working on me.

As a mom of three, I remember there being times where we were preparing to have our last meal. I didn't have any money or food in the house but by the grace of God, we never starved or went without. This happened on several occasions, but my children never knew. There have been times I doubted His existence. The enemy's job is to deceive you of truth; I am a living witness. I am reminded of all the times that we "somehow" had money, "somehow" had food, "somehow" got a bill paid, "somehow" got a roof over our head. Other's might call it luck, but I know that it was nothing but God.

Daily I reflect on how I spiritually used to be versus how I am today. Guess what? There is a difference, and it is continually getting better. I didn't suddenly change, not by any stretch of the imagination. God has been working on me the moment He called me into existence in my mom's womb. Everything I've experienced thus far was for a reason and greater purpose. I know that it sounds CRAZY to say that God "ALLOWED" me to go through things such as rape, suicidal thoughts, promiscuity, homosexuality, fornication, adultery etc., but I don't see it as being crazy. I see it as His preserving my testimony for such a time as this. What I know for a certainty is that I don't regret my past, but instead use it as a testimony that played a major part in making me who and how I am today. Were any of those terrible things good to go through? Not at all, but they were wounds that God was able to heal and deliver me from unto His glory. I now realize how my life was set up to touch more lives of people who may be on the brink of giving up on God or throwing in the towel on life. What I say to those people is "NOT TODAY!" God is real, He is present, He is standing by ready and waiting to hear from you from the depths of your heart and the realness of your soul's plea!

I didn't know it while I was going through, but the strength He placed in me has always operated on a much higher level.

There is a saying that goes "you never know how strong you are until being strong is the only option." When you're down to that last option of strength, you best believe, it is God's strength at work through you! I vouch for that 100 percent! Can you imagine being 14 years old in a house full of guys who wanted nothing more from you than sex and not knowing HOW you will get home? It was nothing but the grace and strength of GOD that allowed me to walk out of that situation, in my right mind, as well as all of the other terrible situations.

The feeling of rejection could have led me to a permanent depressive state. It could have led me to actually act on suicide instead of just having mere thoughts. I tell people all the time, "If you only knew my story, you would understand my GLORY." There have been so many times where I wanted to give up, where I thought life couldn't get any better, or better yet, any worse. There have been many times where I cried in the shower because I didn't think I could go on, "….but Joy came in those mornings." My life isn't completely figured out. My relationship with God needs work and I stand here allowing Him to do what only He can do!

Chapter 24

Doing What I Do

◇◇◇◇◇◇◇◇

N owadays I know better, so I do better. I am still a work in progress, but I try my best to operate by the motto "lead by example." I am focused on my mind, body, and spirit. Life can be so busy at times that you forget to take care of YOU. Working on bettering myself a little each day is what keeps me grounded. I am very intentional with my time. As a parent, I know that life can and will get crazy. You will have your whole day planned and one minor hiccup will offset the entire plan. That can take a major mental toll on you, especially as a single parent. It can leave you feeling discouraged and maybe even a little depressed. Most mornings I am up at 2 am, driving my son to work, and at the gym no later than 3:30am. With me having to drive my son to work, it gives me that extra dose of discipline to get my butt up, dressed, and maintain discipline attending the gym. My workout sessions typically start with listening to some sort of personal development/motivational speech as I perform intense cardio and some minor weightlifting. Some of my favorite motivational personas are Eric Thomas, Jim Rohn, Sara Jakes-Roberts, Steve Harvey and Joel Osteen. The world has enough craziness going on, therefore I choose to start my day off with something positive. I am learning day by day that what you feed your mind is just as important as what you feed your body. Prayer, daily devotionals, and journaling are also a part of my morning routine. This allows me to set the tone for the day ahead.

While some people support my growth and my journey, many question it. I often get questioned, "Why now?", as well as "Why do you feel a need to share your positivity?" My thought would regularly be, "Are you really asking that?" Anyway, I have chosen to use my platform for sharing positive messages to inspire others. The hope I have is to help someone overcome who is currently going through a storm – whether it be extreme like mine, or completely different but equally as important. I share it so the teen moms can know that there is more to life after having a baby so young. You just have to stop going down the road you're on, seek and put God first – trust and build on your relationship with Him as you keep pressing forward. Yes! You might mess up 100 times and have to reset another 100, but try your best to show up with a "giving up is not an option" attitude. I share it for the people who are surrounded by "negative Nancy's." Other people's thoughts and opinions about you don't make you who you are. What God thinks about you is what matters! Your daily walk shouldn't include people-pleasing. I know it gets hard sometimes, especially when you are the type who just want everyone to be happy. Sometimes you have to be bold and unapologetically YOU – regardless of other's opinions about you. If you have pure intentions and a heart after God, things will work out in your favor.

I realize that people are watching and reading my life. Most importantly, I know my children are doing the same. I NEVER want to paint an unrealistic picture or make myself out to be some type of "perfect Patty," because that's NOT ME! My children may not go down the path that I think is best for them and that's okay. All I can do is lead by example, keep a genuine relationship with them and trust God to help me raise them the best I can. I have always been a caring and active parent, but now I am more intentional in my parenting.

Everything I have been praying for is unfolding. I get to walk in my purpose and help people every day! I work as a health and wellness coach with Herbalife. I've been doing that for roughly two years, and I love it! Not only do I get to help people work on their health and body goals, but I also get to be a light in the lives of many who are or have been in a dark place. I get to help them become the very best version of themselves. Aside from our daily sharing of healthy meals, recipes, and workouts, we share personal development videos and take-aways, pray together, encourage one another, and just overall keep the energy positive in our lives. There's nothing like associating with like-minded, positive people who add and receive value in each other's lives, all the while genuinely being yourself.

I also work as a home health aide, and I absolutely love it! I have been in the medical field since 2015. Ignorantly, I've had people refer to me as someone who just "wipes butts." I am not offended by the snide remarks. My heart and prayers go out to them. Healthcare is so much more than just "wiping butts." Yes, I do help people with personal care, but sometimes I am the ONLY person who checks on them, talks to them or just sits and eats dinner with them. I get to serve them and just bring some light to their world; even if it's just for a couple of hours. Being kind comes in many forms. I just let God lead the way and do my best to be kind and respectful to everyone.

Currently, I am one test away from obtaining my real estate license. My pastime is writing, hence how this book came about. I have always loved to write and had dreams and goals of becoming an author, and have pictured myself as one, but didn't really know if it would ever happen. To have that title behind my name is such a blessing because it's an extension of God at work in my life – He is the Author and Finisher of my faith. Writing this book is something that I have been praying to do for such a long time. I had actually placed it on my vision board in 2020 and now it has manifested.

I have been writing since I was in the 3rd grade and was about 8 years old when I won my first writing [poetry] contest. We had to write a poem and draw a picture to match. I won $100. It was a poem about love. I can't recall all the details of the picture, but I do remember very clearly that it had hearts. Just thinking about that statement, I can hear Grandma Ruth now, teasing me (because her memory has always been better than mine) up until her last days. I have written over 100 poems and 5 plays but never took the next step to get them published. Now that I'm making things happen, I am more intentional about my talents and gifts.

My current relationship status is single. Brandon and I reconnected in July 2020, but split August 2021. It came to a point where I no longer wanted to live together unmarried. I didn't want to split, but he had his reasons as to why we should just break up instead of continuing our relationship in separate homes, until marriage. We respectfully went our separate ways but remain in contact every now and again. All in all, the love, friendship, and connection will always be there; it always has been.

As of the completion of this writing, I still haven't officially told my daughters about Brandon and I splitting. Being the oldest, my son knows. By him being naturally nonchalant, it's a bit difficult describing how he may actually feel upon me telling him. He just wants me to be happy and doesn't want us to continue with the cycle of "break up to make up." He also feels as if our relationship is salvageable. My middle child, whew! Although she likes Jaybird, they have never really connected or formed a tight bond, so she pretty much is indifferent when it comes to our relationship. Well, I could only assume so, because she rarely expresses any emotions unless she is mad or irritated about something. My youngest loves her some Jaybird. At the most recent event he came to, she started to call him "Dad"; then proceeded to ask me if I thought he was happy that she called him that. I try my best not to force my own thoughts and opinions on my children, so I told her to ask him herself. He gave her a general answer. I assume he was caught off guard because we are no longer together, and he is not used to her calling him Dad. She has done so in the past, but only for short periods of time. My immediate family loves Jaybird and wants us together FOREVER. We have been divorced since 2018 and he is still invited by family members to all of our family events. I'm not sure if we will ever reconcile for good or if we will one day move on with other people. At this point, it is in God's hands.

Chapter 25

My Encouragement to You

◇◇◇◇◇◇◇◇◇◇◇◇

MAKE IT HAPPEN! Each day that you are blessed to live, strive to be at least one percent better than yesterday. Try to get up 30 minutes earlier. Read one more page of something positive. Do one more set of pushups. Talk to God for a couple of extra minutes. Give the kids an extra kiss on their way to school. As a believer, I spent a lot of time thinking that what you do and accomplish on this earth doesn't matter because it's not your forever home. I beg to differ. How I live my life and pour into others will play a part in their lives after I am gone. I know that death is a touchy and scary subject whether you are a believer or not, and I am NOT speaking death into my life anytime soon; BUT, when it happens, I want to die empty! I want to have laughed, loved, walked in my purpose, helped as many people as I could, and leave a piece of light in their life that is soooo bright, that they won't have room to cry because of my absence.

I know that God is not done with me because He is still waking me up. I want to encourage you to start LIVING life. For a long time, I was just existing. I knew that I was put here on this earth for a reason, but I couldn't quite put my finger on it. I remember my amazing cousin, Owen, messaging me one day telling me that I have the gift of inspiration. He read a post I made and was led to tell me that. I know that I have always been pretty good with words, hence my classmates would ask me to write poems for them to give to their boyfriend/girlfriend. In my adult years, I started realizing that my story could inspire others. It wasn't until this year 2021 that I actually started taking it SERIOUS. My cousin's words stuck with me and replayed in my head on a daily basis.

I do a lot of business on social media. Some of my business partners will ask me to send them my posts and captions and ask me where those words come from? They must be a gift from God. It is very rare that I sit for long periods of time trying to figure out what to say. I don't pretend to be a super deep person, I just speak from the heart. Wow! The gift of inspiration? Not me! I had a baby at 15, lived a very promiscuous lifestyle, have heavily indulged in sinful pleasures and played with fire for many years of my life, now I am out here inspiring people. I am so thankful!

I want to share some things I have learned and been reminded of from my Herbalife training sessions as well as daily personal developments:

- ➤ No matter how bad a situation is, there is still going to be a rose that grows from that dirt.
- ➤ What you practice in private (good or bad), you are rewarded for in public, but you have to put in the work to make it count for something good.

➤ Forget the things you can't control. Look for the moments you can control. Lose the times you can't control. Use the times you can control.

➤ Either you head in the direction you want to go, or you go in no direction at all.

➤ Motivation will get you started; Habit will keep you going.

➤ Nourish your values like a mother and fight your enemies like a father (even the enemies within).

➤ Most people think that the temporary things are permanent things. When you're feeling bad, you think that's how you will feel forever and that's what makes you feel worse.

➤ You will grow through what you go through.

Life does get hard. Sometimes those difficult times may last for a few days and sometimes they may last for years. Some days it is easy to pick yourself up and get through it; other days you will struggle BIG TIME! In the midst of my bad days, I know that God is right there with me. He may let me stumble. He may even let me fall, but He will NOT let me stay there. Life does get scary. Some days my anxiety is CRAZY high. I overthink and worry a LOT! For these reasons, personal development is non-negotiable for me. I do pray and talk to God, but I can't lie to you that things automatically get better after that. There are actions that I must be accountable and responsible for doing to prevent a hostile takeover within my mind. Some days I calm the noise with music or hours of personal development. I have to drown out the thoughts of the enemy.

As I sit here writing this, EVERYTHING I own, besides my clothes, is in a storage unit that I can't afford. I am sitting on my mom's bed in a two-bedroom apartment because I am not in a financial position to get a nice home for my babies and I. My cell phone is off, so I can't check on my team or any of my clients. My car note is due in three days, and I have no idea how I am going to get from this point to the next. Guess what? It's not my business HOW. All I need to know is that it is going to happen, and I need to be ready when it does. One day I will be able to pay my bills up for a year and not worry about having money left over afterwards. I will be able to surprise my children and future husband with our dream home. I will have many Herbalife clients who actually want to take their health and mindset serious and become better versions of themselves. One day I will be selling houses and land, with back-to-back clients as a successful real estate agent. One day I will have several books out and touch many lives with my "gift of inspiration." I know this is not my forever home, but it is where God has me for now. He knows that material things, glitz and glam don't excite me, and I know that He keeps His promises and knows the desires of my heart.

When you feel like giving up, open your eyes! Didn't you wake up today? So, what are you giving up for? God awakened you this morning, so He clearly hasn't given up on you. Learn to walk by faith and not by sight. I have not perfected this, but I try daily. YOUR DAY WILL COME! You just have to continue to believe in yourself, trust God and put in the WORK. Start using your gift(s) and walking in your purpose. I do not care how unimportant or small you or other people THINK it is. If you can knit sweaters, build bicycles from scratch, bake cakes, do hair, fry chicken, paint houses, draw or whatever it is, DO IT! Thank God daily for your gift(s) and do it proudly to the best of your ability EVERY SINGLE DAY! Trust and believe me, while you are downplaying your gift, there is someone out there who wishes they were as talented as you. They wish they had that same talent or ANY talent for that matter!

We have to remember that the conversations that we have with God are private. I am guilty of always wanting to share my goals and dreams. I am not saying never share them, but just know that everyone won't be as excited as you are because they weren't in that conversation between you and God. Also, know that what is shared between you and God needs to stay between you and God. When it manifests, that will be the proof and 'need to know' for others, not me telling them prematurely. Carnal people (including family and friends) look at things with their natural eyes. They may question your plan, your finances, your skills etc. But if God says He is going to teach you HOW to do it and make you successful at it, it doesn't matter how unsupportive others are. I assure you that there are people I used to associate with still hoping and looking for my downfall, still labeling me as a "street woman" and still mad at me for something I did over 18 years ago. Guess what? That has nothing to do with me today. That battle is for God to fight on my behalf. Start prioritizing bettering yourself in every aspect, every single day and watch how your life begin to change. I leave you with this scripture from Matthew 6:33, "But seek first His kingdom and His righteousness, and all these things will be given to you as well."

Chapter 26

Personal Inspirational Thoughts

◇◇◇◇◇◇◇◇◇◇◇◇◇◇

I'd rather be a loner than associate myself with people who try to take me back to the old version of me.

When you start to realize that you deserve better, you'll start to REQUIRE it, and people will either adjust to it or be removed from the equation.

Stop settling for less when God is so much more!

Nowadays I'm very intentional with my time. God is NOT steady waking me up to stay in the same place. I'm learning, practicing, growing and trying to create a better life for my family.

Stop expecting GOD to take you to the next level, when you're unappreciative of the level He currently has you positioned in.

It feels good to feel good. I remember a time where I didn't feel good, where I didn't know what my GIFT or PURPOSE was. NOW I can walk confidently in this crazy world, KNOWING I am here for a REASON. I pray that GOD continues to order my steps and use me to help change and impact lives.

Because at one point, my lifestyle was toxic. I wouldn't want my daughters or anyone else to be like the old me...so excuse me while I vibrate on a higher frequency, walk in my purpose, enjoy my peaceful lifestyle and inspire others to just BE BETTER!

Shout-out to the people who try to dim my light on a daily basis. You all are only making it brighter. God doesn't play about His children.

Life hits different when you count your own blessings instead of counting everyone else's.

Your new life is going to cost you your old one. It's going to cost you your comfort zone and your sense of direction. It's going to cost you relationships and friends. It's going to cost you being liked and understood. But it doesn't matter. Because the people who are meant for you are going to meet you on the other side. And you're going to build a new comfort zone around the things that actually move you forward. Instead of being liked, you're going to be loved. Instead of understanding, you're going to be seen. All you're going to lose is what was built for a person you no longer are. Let it go!

Acknowledgements

◇◇◇◇◇◇◇◇◇◇

First and foremost, I thank GOD! I would not have life or be able to impact lives if it were not for Him. I am thankful for his grace, mercy, and everlasting love.

I would like to thank my parents Brigette Stevenson and Anthony Thomas. Although they separated when I was very young, my bond with each of them is unbreakable. My mother raised me to love God, be kind and respectful. She encourages me daily to keep going, to keep living my truth.

The support I get from my dad, Anthony Thomas, is nothing less than AMAZING. He is honest with me, even if it hurts. He listens without judgement, even if he doesn't agree and although he lives 8 hours away, he makes time for me every single day.

I want to thank my wonderful children; Key' Andre Thomas, Key'Essence Thomas and Bre'Elle Are. My only and favorite son, Key'Andre is my rock. He keeps me laughing and in good spirits, especially on the roughest days. He is always checking on me and

I admire his love and respect for me as his mother. My middle child, Key'Essence, definitely keeps me on my toes. She challenges me to be better. Just when I think I have parenting figured out, here she comes with another challenge. I adore her for being so responsible and helping me grow as a parent. Then there's my baby, Bre'Elle. The one I almost aborted. She is such a bright light in my life. I admire her love for GOD, her positivity, her good energy and sweet spirit. She displays unconditional love on a daily basis and supports me in every way possible.

I would like to thank my partner, Brandon Tyler, for never judging me. I shared my testimony with him early in our relationship and he still treated me the same. I appreciate him for loving me in spite of and not treating me like so many guys have in the past.

I can't forget my Herbalife family. I prayed for a community of people like this and GOD has truly showed up and showed out. They motivate and encourage me on a daily basis to show up! Show up for myself, for my family and just use each GOD given day to improve a little bit more.

I would like to thank Tyneisha Reed for being unapologetically her. Her sharing her story has definitely inspired me to share mine. When we talk, her words exuberate love, encouragement and faith. I truly admire her light.

Last but definitely not least, I would like to thank my cousin, Owen Watson. I thank him for loving me, for encouraging me and being a great addition to my life and to my journey as an author.

Our relationship solidifies that distance doesn't determine your love and support for family.

There are so many people who I've crossed paths with who have, unknowingly, helped mold me into the woman I am today. I am truly thankful for each and every one of them.

Our reluctance to confide in that distance does not hold us back...

There are many people who have shared with us their ... to help ... make the woman I am today. For ... or each and everyone of us ...

Author Antoinette Thomas

OTHER BOOKS OFFERED BY

Turn the Page in Your Life

Prayers for Life's Journey

Betting on Me: Revelatory Concepts
for Success

Defeating Cancer One Poem a Day

Po' Man Ain't Got Not Much Say

What Matters Most: Family, Friends,
and Foes